Alone on the High Seas to Scotland

Bill Howland

For Denise & Mike

Thank you for all the good work
with my Granddaughter Kayla.

All the best.

Bill Howland

11-14-2014

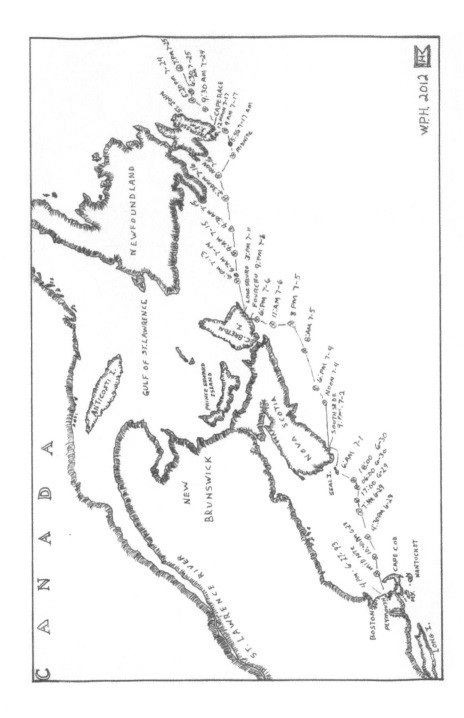

DEDICATION

To Jim MacDonald,
who is sorely missed.

August 4, 1952 - December 11, 2003

ACKNOWLEDGEMENTS

This journal would not have been published without the enthusiasm of my good friend, Phil Williams, who guided me relentlessly, as the good coach he is.

Seeing something I did not,
Blinded by my train of thought,
Opening old eyes to see,
A different side of me.

I am grateful to Jim Robb, Phil Williams, Elayna Collin, for their editing skills. To Christine Lemay and Michelle Lemay of Morningstar Design, Falmouth, Ma. for their part in bringing this book into fruition. And, to my stepsister, Debbie Ripely, who sewed up the canvas cloths and house flag. And, much appreciation to the Plymouth Yacht Club for their hospitality, and others who so graciously helped me along this journey.

Note on the Text

What the reader sees is an exact photo copy of Bill
Howland's original journal. The original is squirreled away
in a safe deposit box. The copy is on the right hand page.
On the left hand page is a printed version of the journal
which has been edited to bring clarity to readers.
The printed version was originally set up by Elayna Collin,
nineteen years after the journal was written. Her set-up allows
one to read the journal mostly page for page, line for line and
word for word.*
Bill wrote the original journal just about every day of the
voyage as he was aboard the Kandahar.** Some days he
wrote in the cockpit. Some days, below deck in the cabin,
and during the stormiest days he wrote while braced in a bean
bag chair lying on the cabin sole. This explains the different
forms of penmanship, the multiple use of commas to
punctuate his changing thoughts, the scratches, the
misspellings, the different pens used, and so on.
The printed version is mostly the result of two friends studying
the hand written journal while seated at a stable dinning room
table in a comfortable home. They had the leisure to argue about
what they thought Bill meant with his off-hand scribbling. The
arguments were long and contentious, but nothing like Bill's cre-
ation of the journal. The editing was a lot of fun, and gave much
satisfaction to us.

* Except with poems
** Except in instances where I later made
corrections, in order to bring forth factual
information. These corrections are noted
by an astrick and italics.
Also, all drawings (created in 2012) were
added to enhance the readers experience
of my voyage.

Phil Williams and Jim Robb
Falmouth, Massachusetts
July 30, 2012

- Wm. Howland

Published by
LuLu

Cover Art & Interior Drawings by William Howland

Library of Congress Cataloging-in-Publication Data

Howland, Bill.
  Alone on the High Seas to Scotland / Bill Howland
    p. cm.
  ISBN 978-1-304-57558-6
  I. Title

First Edition: 2013
10 9 8 7 6 5 4 3 2 1

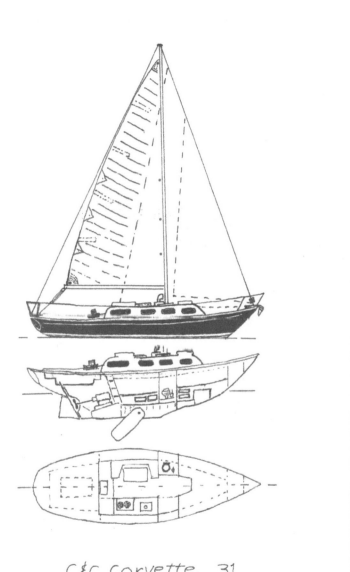

C&C Corvette 31

6-27-1993 Sunday
1600 hrs. (4 PM)
Finally got underway today from the dock
at Plymouth Yacht Club.
Weather is hazy. Overcast is high.
Visibility is ok. I can see the Gurnet
ok. Temp. about 70° F. John is at the helm.
We are motoring to at least clear of
the harbor and the Gurnet.
Where the last few days saw a stiff
breeze out of the s.w. at 20-25, today it's
a mill pond.
It's late in the afternoon but I feel
the need to go, to get started, feeling
anxious.
Halfway out of the harbor we were
overtaken by one of the clubs' skiffs with
my Aunt Peg aboard. She handed over the
rail to me two bags of groceries with a happy
but concerned look on her face.
"If you're going, or feel you have to, then be
careful!" she yelled above the sound of
the engines. John remained at the helm
and continued to make headway in the
narrow channel.
Dexter McNeil at the helm of the

6-??-1993   Sunday
1600 hrs. (4 PM)
Finally got under way today from the dock
at Plymouth Yacht Club.
Weather is hazy, overcast in high,
visability is ok I can see the Gurnet
etc, temp. about 70°F John is at the helm,
we are motoring to at least clear of
the harbor and the Gurnet.
Where the last few days saw a stiff
breeze out of the ene at 20-25, today its
a quiel wind
It's late in the afternoon but I feel
the need to go, to get started, feeling
anxious.
Half way out of the harbor we were
overtaken by one of the Clubs skiffs with
my Aunt Peg aboard, she handed over the
rail to me two bags of groceries with a happy
but concerned look on her face.
"If your going, or feel you have to, then be
carefull" she yelled, above the sound of
the engines. John remained at the helm
and continued to make headway in the
narrow channel.
Dexter McNeil at the helm of the

2

skiff put his engine in neutral, and slowly
we began to move away from them.
As we pass Bug Light and begin to enter
Cape Cod Bay, I can't keep my eyes off
of Plymouth. My thoughts return me
to the fond memories of times spent there,
in the past year; of last summer living
aboard Kandahar on a yacht club mooring.
Of the early morning trips across the harbor,
dodging the wakes of fishermen and lobstermen
making their way to and fro in pursuit
of their daily bread. And me too, making my
way to the dinghy dock then to the parking
lot, hopping in my van and beginning the
hour long trek into Boston; to Beacon Hill
where I spent that time working my
trade as a carpenter.
 Phil Williams was there with his son
"Flip", and what a grand time we had
gutting out and remodeling one of those
grand, old stately residences.
 Phil and I go back 8 or 9 years and
he was the inspiration for me to buy
a "sail" boat in the first place, but
not exactly a "fiberglass" one.

3

skiff put his engine in neutral and slowly
we began to move away from them.
As we pass Bug light and begin to enter
Cape Cod bay I can't keep my eyes off
of Plymouth, and my thoughts return me
to the fond memories of times spent there
in the past year, of last summer living
aboard Kandahar on a yacht club mooring,
of the early morning trips across the harbor
dodging the wakes of fishermen and lobster—
men making their way to and fro in pursuite
of their daily bread. And me too, making my
way to the dinghy dock then to the parking
lot hopping in my van and beginning the near
hour long treck into Boston to Becon Hill
where I spent that time working my
trade as a carpenter.
    Phil Williams was there with his son
"Filip" and what a grand time we had
gutting out and remodeling one of those
grand old statley residences.
    Phil and I go back 8 or 9 years and
he was the inspector for me to buy
a "sail" boat in the first place but
not exactly a "fiberglass" one.

4

Bug Light

w.e.H. 2012

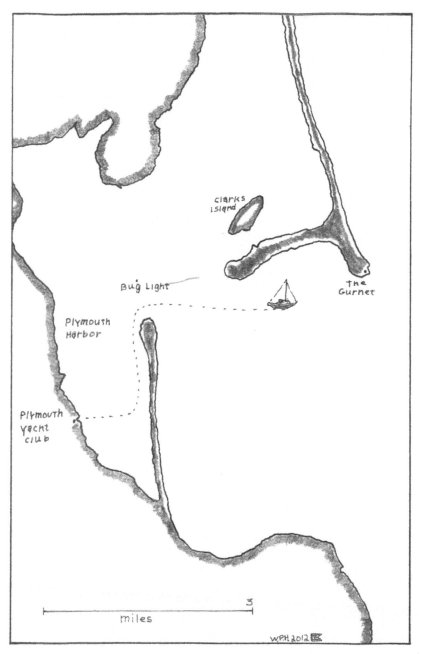

Clarks Island

Bug Light

The Gurnet

Plymouth Harbor

Plymouth Yacht Club

3

miles

W.P.H. 2012

6

Phil is more of an "old school" sailor.
One who prefers to be seen on a classic
wooden vessel. And, in the course of the
four years I've owned Kandahar only once
did he agree to go for a small jaunt
with me aboard her.
 Even so, Phil and I spent many a happy
time together, and it's to Phil I owe
what ever I know about boats and sailing.
 As we clear the Gurnet, I give John
a new heading so that we clear the
tip of Cape Cod, just over the horizon
to the east. I hope to be clear of the
Cape and offshore a few miles before the
night closes in. I also have in the back
of my mind, that if need be, Provincetown harbor
would be handy for "second thoughts".
 It's about 3000 nautical miles from Plymouth
to Largs, Scotland and I figure in my head
to make least 100 miles a day (or in 24 hrs.).
That's 30 days give or take a few. That
should bring me to July 29th, the date
that Jim MacDonald will be arriving there.
I'm probably nuts, but it seemed at the time
of my decision, a what the hell, why not,

Phil is more of an "old school" sailor -
one who prefered to be seen on a classic
wooden vessel and in the course of the
four years I've owned Kandahar only once
did he agree to go for a small jaunt
with me aboard her.

Evan so Phil and I spent many a happy
time togeather and it's to Phil I owe
whatever I know about boats and sailing.

As we clear the Gurnet I give John
a new heading so that we clear the
lip of Cape Cod just over the horizon
to the east. I hope to be clear of the
Cape and off shore a few miles before the
night closes in. I also have in the back
of my mind that, if need be, Provence Town harbor
would be handy for "second thoughts".

It's about 3000 nautical miles from Plymouth
to Largs, Scotland and I figure in my head
to make at least 100 miles a day (or in 24 hrs.)
That's 30 days give or take a few. That
should bring me to July 29th the date
that Jim MacDonald will be arriving there.
I'm probably nuts but it seemed at the time
of my decision a what the hell, why not,

8

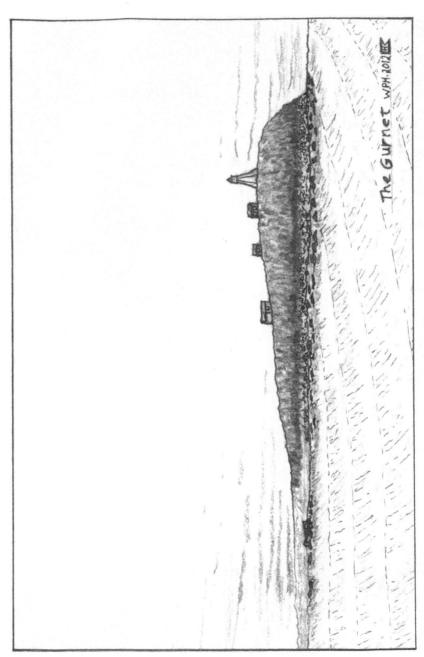

The Gurnet WPH. 2012

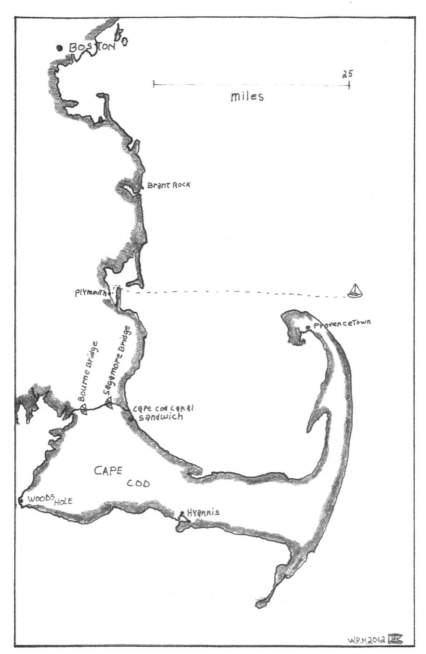

BOSTON

25

miles

Brant Rock

Plymouth

Provencetown

Bourne Bridge

Sagamore Bridge

Cape Cod Canal
Sandwich

CAPE

COD

WOODS HOLE

Hyannis

W.P.H 2012

adventure.

It all started just a month ago, five weeks
actually, when Jim and I were working together,
something he and I have done on and off for
about ten years. Jim is from Scotland and
has a lovely brogue and a peach of a personality.
Each day in his presence was a pleasant one.
We would get a lot of work done, whistling
along to the oldies of the 50's & 60's, often
taking a half day off to play some golf.
Jim loved golf even though neither one
of us was very good at it. Jim always
beat me by at least 10 or more strokes,
but the friendship was worth every minute
of his bantering.

"Marilyn and the kids and I are going to
Scotland in late July for two weeks," he
said to me one day. "Why don't you come over
and check out Scotland while we're there?"

My God, I thought to myself, would I love
to do that. "Yeah," I said. "That sounds like fun."
What was I to do? "I'm sure Dad would love
to see ya," he said. I met his dad last
summer when he came to visit Jim for
a month and Jim brought him to work

adventure.

It all started just a month ago, five weeks actually when Jim and I were working togeather something he and I have done on and off for about ten years. Jim is from Scotland and has a lovely broge and a peach of a personality. Each day in his presents was a pleasant one. We would get a lot of work done, whistling along to the oldies of the 50's & 60's, often taking a half day off to play some golf. Jim loved golf even though neither one of us was very good at it. Jim always beat me by at least 10 or more strokes but the friendship was worth every minute of his bantering.

"Marilyn and the kids and I are going to Scotland in late July for two weeks," he said to me one day, "why don't you come over and check out Scotland while were there".

My God, I thought to myself would I love to do that. "Yeah" I said "that sounds like fun". What was I to do? "I'm sure Dad would love to see ya" he said. I met his dad last summer when he came to visit Jim for a month and Jim brought him to work

12

with him so he wouldn't be hanging around
the house all day. It was great to have him
around for the time he was here and we
all got along like family.

During his time here I received an invitation
from Holty Wood, down the cape in Catumet,
to race in what he calls "The Invitational
Gentlemen's Yacht Race." This was my third
invitation to, what I feel, a terrifically fun event.
"For Yachts with Character and Characters with
Yachts', reads the official invitation with
accompanying procedures and rules.

I invited Jim and his father
along as crew for the race. We had a grand
time. The society ladies there hovered
around old Jim, and he was the star guest
at the post-race reception for Captains and
crew.

"I'd love to go the Scotland, Jim. About how
much is the flight?" "About six hundred dollars
round trip to Glasgow," he said. "That would
be great. I'm going over and spend a week
there before Marilyn and the kids arrive.
Why don't you come then?"

This was a lot to think about.

with him so he wouldn't be hangin around
the house all day. It was great to have him
around for the time he was here and we
all got along like family.

During his time here I recieved an invitation
from Holty Wood down the cape in Catumet
to race in what he calls "The Invitational
Gentlemen's Yacht Race". This was my third
invitation to, what I feel, a terifically fun event.
"For Yachts with Character and Character with
Yachts". reads the official invitation with
accompanying procedures and rules.

I invited Jim and his ~~partner~~ father
along as "crew" for the race, we had a grand
time and the society ladies there hovered
around old Jim and he was the star guest
at the post race reception for Captains and
crew.

"I'd love to go to Scotland Jim about how
much is the flight" "about six hundred dollars
round trip to Glasgow" he said "that would
be great. I'm going over and spend a week
there before Marilyn and the kids arrive
why don't you come then?"

This was a lot to think about

14

"I'll let you know in a few days," I said.
"Don't wait too long," he said. "The planes fill up
pretty fast in the summer."
 The next day I told him I am going
to sail Kandahar over and meet him.
He thought I was crazy, and maybe so
I am.
 I had just sold a piece of land that
was on the market for two years
in New Hampshire. Part of a settlement
in a separation, a painful one for
both of us, but one of my initiation.
Eight thousand dollars. More than enough
I thought to get Kandahar ready and take
the time off to do the trip.
 I replaced the lower mast stays, bought
two new batteries, a life raft, an EPIRB, engine
spare parts, put 3 reef points in the mainsail,
and had a sail maker check out my three sails
as to their condition: a main, a genoa jib
and a working jib. I made up some panels
out of canvas for spray shields and attached
them to both port and starboard life lines.
 The running rigging seemed in pretty good
shape only being a few years old.

15

"I'll let you know in a few days" I said "don't wait too long" he said "the planes fill up pretty fast in the summer".

The next day I told him I am going to sail Kandahar over and meet him. He thought I was crazy and maybe so I am.

I had just sold a piece of land that ~~there~~ was on the market for two years in New Hampshire. Part of a settlement in a separation, a painfull one for both of us but one of my ~~own~~ initiation. Eight thousand dollars, more than enough I thought to get Kandahar ready and take the time off to do the trip.

I replaced the lower most stays, bought two new batteries, a life raft, an eperb, engine spare parts, put 3 reef points in the mainsail, had a sail maker check out my ~~three~~ sails ~~too~~ as to their condition, a main, a genoa jib and a working jib. I made up some panels out of canvis for spray shields and attached them to both port and starbord life lines. The running rigging seemed in pretty good shape only being a few years old.

16

Kandahar is twenty-four years old but
reasonably cared for by her previous owners.
A thirty-one foot sloop built in Canada
by *Cuthbertson and *Cassion, "C&C", in 1969,
of hand-laid fiberglass. Although her hull
is only about one quarter to three-eights of an
inch thick, she is sound, and I feel, sea-
worthy. A "Corvette" shoal-draft racing-
cruiser, with centerboard down she draws
seven feet of water and with centerboard up,
less than four.
 At first sight I was hooked on her charms.
With graceful shear and overhanging stern,
classic styling. I thought I was
truly blessed to be able to afford such
a fine craft as she is.

6-27-1993   20:00 HRS (8 PM)   42-40 N 68-27 w
I relieved John at the helm. Took a LORAN
reading just before. Still daylight. Haven't
reached the outer tip of the cape yet.
Very light breeze, 5-7 probably. Should have
run the engine but am saving the fuel
for the time I might really need it.
Have *15 gallons in the tank and 2 five

Kandahar ~~is~~ twenty four years old but
reasonably cared for by her previous owners.
A thirty one foot sloop built in Canada
by Cuthbertson and Cassian "C&C" in 1969
of hand laid fiber glass. Although her hull
~~is~~ only about one quarter to three eights of an
inch thick. she ~~is~~ sound and I felt sea
worthy. A "Corvette" shoal draft racing —
cruiser, with center board down she draws
seven feet of water and with center board up
less ~~than~~ four.

    At first sight I was ~~hooked~~ on her charm
with a gracefull shear and overhanging stearn
classic, ~~~~, styling. I thought I was
truely blessed to be able to afford such
a fine ~~craft~~ as she is.

6-27-1993   20:00 HRS (8 PM)   42-40ᴺ 68-27ᵂ
I relieved John at the helm. Took a LORAN
reading just before. Still daylight haven't
reached the outer tip of the cape yet
Very light breeze 5-7 probably should have
run the engine but am saving the fuel
for the time I might really need it.
Have 15 gal. in the tank and 2 five

gallon jerry cans stowed in the chain locker
on top of the anchor rode. Don't think I'll
need an anchor for a while.
The one cylinder Yanmar diesel pushes us
along at 5 knots or so full throttle and
about 4 knots at 3/4 throttle. I put on
a 3 blade prop after realizing I couldn't
make the passage through Woods Hole
with a full current running, swinging
the two bladed prop.
 John went immediately down below to his
V-birth and closed the door behind him.
A feeling of apprehension comes over me.
He really doesn't want to be here. I've done
the best I know how to reassure him
that we'll be ok, but he is very intuitive
to my feelings, and may be feeling my
anxiety.
 Four hours on and four off, that is
the system I've begun with, but I can't
even imagine doing it straight for 30 days.
Whatever possessed me to think that
he and I could even manage this in
the first place?

gal. jerry cans stowed in the chain locker on top of the anchor rode, don't think I'll need an anchor for a while.

The one cylinder Yanmar diesel pushes us along at 5 knots or so full throttle and about 4 knots at 3/4 throttle. I put on a 3 blade prop, after realizing I couldn't make the passage through Woods Hole, with a full current running, swinging the two bladed prop.

John went immediatly down below to his vee birth and closed the door behind him. A feeling of aprehension comes over me. He really doesn't want to be here. I've done the best I know how to reasure him that we'll be o.k. but he is very intuitive to my feelings and may be feeling my anxiety.

Four hours on and four off, that is the system I've begune with but I can't even imagine doing it straight for 30 days. What ever possesed me to think that he and I could ever manage this in the first place.

6-28-1993
24:00 Midnight   42.17 69:58   Course 84° M
No wind, I started the engine just after
taking the helm, around 8:30. Turned
about 4 knots. John seemed irritable
when I called him for watch. The
visibility is poor, a few miles. Two fishing
vessels passed to port about an hour ago.
With no wind at all it was too risky just
sitting around this close to shore only
about 18 mi. off the tip of the Cape.
I feel uneasy about going down below for
some shut eye but here I am. Got to close
my eyes for a little while though. I'm
pooped.

08:20 AM   6-28-1993
John woke me at 04:00 for my watch. Slept
like a log. Still motoring. Have no idea how
much fuel we have used, no gauge. I remember
one night two years ago motoring west in
the Cape Cod Canal, on my way back from
a week cruising the coast of Maine. I pulled
into the marina on the Sandwich end.
It's a small affair, and popular, and full up
in the season. Midnight, the tide was
running east at a pretty good clip.

6-28-1993

24:00 MIDNIGHT   42-17 69:58   COURSE 84° M

No wind, I started the engine just after
taking the helm, around 8:30, turned
about 4 knots, John seemed irritable
when I called him for watch. The
visability is poor, a few miles, two fishing
vessels passed to port about an hour ago.
With no wind at all it was to risky just
sitting around this close to shore only
about 18 mi. of the tip of the Cape.
I feel uneasy about going down below for
some shut eye but here I am, got to close
my eyes for a little while though, I'm
pooped.

08:20 AM 6-28-1993

John woke me at 04:00 for my watch, slept
like a log, still motoring, have no idea how
much fuel we have used, no gage. I remember
one night two years ago motoring west in
the Cape Cod canal. On my way back from
a week crusing the coast of Maine. I pulled
into the marina on the Sandwich end,
its a small affair, and popular, and full up
in the season. Midnight, the tide was
running east at a pretty good clip,

22

Thought it would be a good idea to pull in
and rest till morning. Fuel pumps were
shut down, it was pretty quiet. The only
place to tie up was to the dock by the
boat ramp. Came along side and tied up,
shut down the engine and was sitting in
the cockpit listening to the quiet of not
having it running, feeling the relief.
 Sally, my mate at the time, was down
below, snoozing away. She and I had done
six on and six off all the way from
Isle Au Haut, 24-something hours, motoring
most of the way into a light breeze.
As soon as the engine stopped she was
awakened by the quiet and came up to
see where we were. No sooner than
she sat down for a moment a loud
voice rang out, "Hey you on the ramp
dock, get out of here, you can't tie up
there!" I looked out in the darkness
in the direction from where I thought
the voice came from and saw a large
silhouette coming down the dock.
"You can't stay here!" he said in a loud voice
over again. "I pulled in to wait for the

thought it would be a good idea to pull in
and rest till morning. Fuel pumps were
shut down, it was pretty quiet, the only
place to tie up was to the dock by the
boat ramp. Came along side and tied up,
shut down the engine and was sitting in
the cockpit listening to the quiet of not
having it running, feeling the relief.
Sally, my Mate at the time, was down
below snoozing away, she and I had done
a six on and six off all the way from
Isle A Haught, something hours, motoring
most of the way into a light breeze.
As soon as the engine stopped she was
awakened by the quiet and came up to
see where we were. No sooner than
she sat down for a moment a loud
voice rang out, "Hey you on the ramp
dock get out of here, you can't tie up
there". I looked out in the darkness
in the direction from where I thought
the voice came from and saw a large
silouett comming down the dock.
"You can't stay here" he said in a loud voice
over again. I pulled in to wait for the

24

tide and for the fuel docks to open in
the morning," but before I finished explaining
anything else he interrupted and said, "Doesn't
matter what you pulled in here for you
can't stay. Start her up and be gone."
"You mean you want me to go back
out there in the canal with the current
running against me with eight miles
to go before the next safe harbor with
little fuel?" "I don't care where you go,"
he said. "Long as you get your boat off
this dock right now!" "Do you have
a slip for the night then?" I said to him,
and he replied, "No, nothin' here."
So, I started up, cast off and left.
Once out in the canal I told Sally to
go back down below and get some rest,
I'll be alright, and so she did.
I nearly made it to the entrance to
Buttermilk Bay, just a couple of miles
to go. A hundred yards or so beyond
the large concrete piers that support
the legs of the Bourne Bridge the
engine stopped. My God, what a panic!
There I was out of fuel, being pushed

tide and for the fuel docks to open in
the morning," but before I finished explaining
anything else he interrupted and said "doesn't
matter what you pulled in here for you
can't stay, start her up and be gone".
"You mean you want me to go back
out there in the canal with the current
running against me with eight miles
to go before the next safe harbor with
little fuel." "I don't care where you go
he said long as you get your boat off
of this dock right now." "Do you have
a slip for the night then" I said to him
and he replied "No, nothin' here".
So I started up, cast off and left.
Once out in the canal I told Sally to
go back down below and get some rest,
I'll be alright, and so she did.
I nearly made it to the entrance to
Buttermilk Bay, just a couple of miles
to go, a hundred yards or so beyond
the large concrete piers that support
the legs of the ~~Sagamore~~ Bourne bridge the
engine stopped. My God what a panic,
there I was out of fuel being pushed

26

rapidly towards the one (pillar) on the mainland
side. I don't think I've ever moved as
fast in my life. Running forward I untied
the anchor and pulled up on deck as
much of the 3/4" nylon rode and chain
as I could and threw all of it at
once over the side, then pulled frantically
the rest of the rode up out of the deck
hole, all 200 or so feet. When that was
done I ran down below and called
on channel 16 "May Day, May Day, this
is Kandahar, I've just lost power in
the canal west of the Bourne Bridge,
over." The response was instantaneous.
"Kandahar this is Canal Control. Boat on
its way." I remember confirming their
reply and rushed topsides to see where
we were going to hit the rocks. All the
time down below I was looking out the
side ports and watching the yellow lights
going by, but as soon as I got topsides
I noticed the current rushing
by us and we were staying in one
spot. The plow anchor somehow had caught
in the rocky bottom and the rode was

rapidly towards the one on the mainland side. I don't think I've ever moved as fast in my life. Running forward I untied the anchor and pulled up on deck as much of the 3/4" nylon rode and chain as I could and threw all of it at once over the side, then pulled frantically the rest of the rode up out of the deck hole all 200 or so feet. When that was done I ran down below and called on chanel 16 "May Day, May Day, this is Kandahar I've just lost power in the canal west of the ~~Sagamore~~ Bourne bridge over." The response was instantainous, Kandahar this is Canal control, boat on it's way. I remember confirming their replay and rushed topsides to see where we were going to hit the rocks, all the time down below I was looking out the side ports and watching the yellow lights ~~going~~ by but as soon as I got topsides ~~and~~ I noticed ~~that~~ the currant rushing by us and we were staying in one spot. The plow anchor some how had caught in the rocky bottom and the ~~rode~~ was

running tight and straight off the bow.
 The canal boat was there in a moment,
tossed me a line and as soon as I had it
on the cleat, off she went and began to
tow us. I reached for the anchor rode and
began to pull it up on deck as fast
as I could with the slack, though it
began to drift astern of me. And then
because the tow boat was going so fast
I couldn't bring it all aboard fast enough,
and soon the anchor was dragging
behind us, and I just managed to get
the part of the rode I had in my hands
around the bow cleat before it pulled
me overboard. There, what a sight!
We were almost on a plane, and a 100 feet
back was my plow anchor, skipping
along in our wake. What an idiot I
was to not carry a spare can of fuel.
Now I feel like an idiot again for not
carrying more than the two 5 gallon cans
in the anchor chain locker.
 Fog set in and was pretty thick at
4 AM.

running tight and straight off the bow.
The canal boat was there in a moment,
tossed me a line and as soon as I had it
on the cleat off she went and began to
tow us, I reached for the anchor rode and
began to pull it up on deck as fast
as I could, with the slack though it
began to drift astern of me and then
because the tow boat was going so fast
I couldn't bring it all aboard fast enough
and soon the anchor was dragging
behind us and I just managed to get
the part of the rode I had in my hands
around the bow cleat before it pulled
me over board. There, what a sight,
we were almost on plane and a 100 feet
back was my plow anchor skipping
along in our wake. What an idiot I
was to not carry a spare can of fuel.
Now I feel like an idiot again for not
carrying more than the two 5 gal. cans
in the anchor chain locker.
   Fog set in and was pretty thick at
4: Am

6-28-1993   10:40 AM   42.19 69.12
 About 50 miles off the coast of Cape
Cod: still no wind. Sky's beginning to
clear out. At this rate I, or we, rather, will
have to stop in Nova Scotia to restock
fuel supplies. I thought I wouldn't need
to use the engine much before getting
close to Scotland.
 Neither John or I are very talkative.
Fourteen hours of motor sailing. The genoa
jib is rolled up and the main is flapping away,
looking for a puff. It's like a mill pond
out here, all alone.

                                                      LORAN
6-28-1993   4:30 PM 16:30 HRS   42.29   68.32

The wind picked up just before my watch
at noon and is blowing about 20+. Genoa
and main, wing and wing, down wind.
Killed the engine. About 75 miles off the
tip of Cape Cod and 100 from Plymouth.
One full day; 29 more to go.

6-28-1993   10:40 AM   42-19   69-12

    About 50 miles off the coast of Cape
Cod still no wind, skys beginning to
clear out, at this rate I, or we rather, will
have to stop in Nova Scotia to re-stock
fuel supplies. I thought I wouldn't need
to use the engine much before getting
close to Scotland.

    Neither John or I are very talkative.
Fourteen hours of motor sailing, the genoa
jib is rolled up and the main is flapping away
looking for a puff. It's like a mill pond
out here, all alone.

6-28-1993   4:30 PM 16:30 HRS.   42.29   LORAN 68.32

The wind picked up just before my watch
at noon and is blowing about 20+. Genoa
and main, wing and wing, down wind,
killed the engine. About 75 miles off the
tip of Cape Cod and 100 from Plymouth,
one full day, 29 more to go

32

6-29-1993   07:00   42.46 67.36

 My watch. The sun has come up but I
can't see it. The wind died last evening,
didn't even have 6 hours of it. We've passed
the halfway point to Nova Scotia. It's a
mill pond again, and foggy and damp and
I've decided not to start the engine, just
drifting and drifting and drifting. If this is what
the weather is going to be like all the way across
it will take us 2 months. Very frustrating!
09:00
 John took the watch at 8, and the sky opened
up on him. We're not going anywhere, and
it's pouring, pouring, pouring. He left the
wheel and dove down to his bunk. I'm
sitting in the cockpit under the dodger, keeping
watch, sorta, can't see a thing and the rain
is making such a racket can't hear anything
else. It's beating the boat and the surrounding
water, like being under a waterfall.
6 PM
 Haven't seen John all day. The rain has slowed
to a drizzle. Still foggy, no wind, made
about 75 mi. in the last 24 hours. Started
up the engine, altered course toward Nova Scotia.

6-29-1993   02:00   42.46   67.36

My watch, the sun has come up but I
can't see it. The wind died last evening,
didn't even have 6 hours of it. We've passed
the half way point to Nova Scotia, it's a
mill pond again and foggy and damp and
I've decided not to start the engine, just
drifting and drifting and drifting, if this is what
the weather is going to be like all the way accross
it will take us 2 months. Very frustrating!

09:00
John took the watch at 8 and the sky opened
up on him, we're not going anywhere and
it's pouring, pouring, pouring. He left the
wheel and dove down to his bunk, I'm
sitting in the cockpit under the dodger, keeping
watch, sorta, can't see a thing and the rain
is making such a racket can't hear anything
else. It's beating the boat and the surrounding
water, like being under a waterfall.

6: PM
Haven't seen John all day, the rain has slowed
to a drizzle, still foggy, no wind, made
about 75 mi in the last 24 hours, started
up the engine, altered course towards Nova Scotia.

34

Got to do something, perhaps find a port
to replenish the fuel we've used.

got to do something, perhaps find a port
to replenish the fuel we've used.

Wed.   N   W
6-30-93   06:00   42-44   66-52
Six a.m. Foggy, drizzle, miserable.
John is not talking.
 I'm really discouraged. Things are not going
anywhere near what I expected.
Thought I'd get some wind by now, something
steady, but instead only a few
hours at a time and then nothing; nothing
but fog and drizzle. I thought John and
I would have some fun and conversation
but to no avail. We're both having a miserable
time and it shows in our dispositions.
1 PM
 What a miserable father I am. I don't
know anything about John. I was hoping
this journey would be a great chance
for us to get to know each other, ya
know, find some way to bond at a deeper
level or something. I just keep making
the same mistakes, what ever they are.
I'm just not aware of how I am turning
him away from me. He just sits there
with his walkman plugged into his
ears. Won't even have eye contact with
me. I feel as if I am observing a
wild animal penned in a cage. I feel

Wed.
6-30-93   06:00   N 42-44   W 66-52

Six a.m. foggy, drizzle, miserable,
John is not talking.
 I'm really discouraged things are not going
anywhere near what I expected.
Thought I'd get some wind by now, something steady but instead only a few
hours at a time and then nothing, nothing
but fog and drizzle. I thought John and
I would have some fun and conversation
but to no avail we're both having a miserable
time and it shows in our dispositions.

1:PM

 What a miserable father I am. I don't
know anything about John. I was hoping
this journey would be a great chance
for us to get to know each other, ya
know, find some way to bond at a deeper
level or something. I just keep making
the same mistakes, what ever they are,
I'm just not aware of how I am turning
him away from me. He just sits there
with his walkman plugged into his
ears, won't even have eye contact with
me. I feel as if I am observing a
wild animal pened in a cage. I feel

38

it's my fault he is here and I'm feeling miserable about the whole situation.

Why am I doing this?

its my fault he is here and I'm feeling
miserable about the whole situation.
Why am I doing this?

6-30-1993   18:00 HRS   6 PM 4   2-58 N   66-31 w
Rain, no wind all day, cool.
John is at the helm. I'm down below in the
port bunk sipping soup (Progresso Split Pea)
with bread & butter.
Another miserable day!!
Thoughts in my head going round and round.
What possesses a man to think his
thoughts are sound ones?
Enough crap, so
much crap in my head.

7-1-1993   06:00 HRS   43-22 N 66-07 W
At daybreak noticed a lighthouse.
Thought it to be Cape Sable, NS. Great sunrise.
Came down below to take a LORAN reading.
Looks to me were off a small island
about as big as a pencil point on the
chart I have. Can't see land, only lighthouse.
Must have drifted north of our
set course over the last 12 hours.
Visibility good, rain cleared out, cool,
a guess of 45-50° F, as have no thermometer.
Reset course to 112° to get
back to my rhumb line and way
point #1 to clear southern NS.

6. 6-30-93   18:00 HRS.   6:PM   42:58 66:31

Rain, no wind all day, cool.
John is at the helm, I'm down below in the
port bunk sipping soup (progresso split pea)
with bread & butter.
Another miserable day!!
Thoughts in my head going round and round,
what ~~poses~~ possess a man to think his
thoughts are sound ones?
~~I wonder~~ over and over, Enough crap, so
much crap in my head.

7-1-93   06:00   43°.22 66°.07
At daybreak noticed a light house,
thought it to be Cape Sable, N.S.
Came down below to take a Loran reading.
Looks to me we are off a small island
about as big as a pencil point on the
chart I have. Can't see land, only light
house. Must have drifted north of our
set course over the last 12 hours.
visability good, rain cleared out, cool,
a guess of 45-50° F as have no thermom-
-ater. Reset course to 112° to get
back to my rube line and way
point # 1 to clear southern N.S.

GREAT SUNRISE

42

7-1-1993 12:00 Noon

John came up on deck just after I
changed course.
"What's going on?" he said, and I told
him what a beautiful sunrise. And, when
he looked he saw the lighthouse.
"Head for that light house!" he said with
determination in his voice. "I'm getting
off." "What do you mean you're getting off?"
was my reply, and he said, "You heard me,
I'm getting off here!"
 With that said, down below he dove
and in a minute was back on deck
with his green army surplus duffel
bag. "Head for that lighthouse."
"But John!" I said, "You can't get off
here! I don't even know where that lighthouse
is . . . looks like it might be on
an island!" "I don't care where it is,
there's land somewhere over there and
that's where I'm going!" he said.
I continued to put up resistance to the
idea but then he had pulled in the
pram dinghy we were towing astern,
threw in his stuff, climbed
over the rail, and was in it.

7-1-95 12 noon

John came up on deck just after I
changed course
"What's goin on" he said. And I told
him what a beautiful sun rise and when
he looked he saw the light house.
"Head for that light house" he said with
determanation in his voice, "I'm getting
off". "What do you mean your getting off"
was my reply and he said "you heard me
I'm getting off here".
With that said down below he dove
and in a minute was back on deck
with his green army surplus duffel
bag. "Head for that light house".
"But John" I said you can't get off
here I don't even know where that light
house is, looks like it might be on
an island". "I don't care where it is,
there's land somewhere over there and
that's were I'm going" he said.
I continued to put up resistance to the
idea but then he had pulled in the
pram dingy we were towing astern,
threw in his stuff and climbed
over the rail and was in it

44

The only chart I have of this area,
the southern tip of Nova Scotia,
is one of the entire North Atlantic. I can
cover up all of Nova Scotia with my
thumb. I hadn't planned on stopping
here!
John insisted I started up the engine
and headed in closer. About two
hours later I was picking my way
through an area of large rocks &
boulders. Depth sounder shows
twenty feet. Kandahar draws four
and the rocks around here average
twenty. I guess the shore line
to be about a half mile or less, and
put the transmission in neutral.
John says "thanks", and began to
row his dinghy towards the shore.
The seas were running three to four foot
swells and I could see them breaking on
what looked like a pretty deserted
rock strewn beach. Not a sign of life
or buildings besides the lighthouse.
Choked up with grief as I made
my way off shore leaving him behind.

The only chart I have of this area,
the southern tip of Nova Scocia,
is one of the entire North Atlantic, I can
cover up all of Nova Scocia with my
thumb. I hadn't planed on stopping
here!

John insisted; I started up the engine
and headed in closer. About two
hours later I was picking my way
through an area of large rocks &
boulders, depth sounder showed ~~its~~
twenty feet. Kandahar draws four
and the rocks around here average
twenty. I guess the shore line
to be about a half mile or less and
put the transmission in netural.

John says thanks and began to
row his dingy towards the shore.
swells The seas were running three to four feet
and I could see them breaking on
what looked like a pretty deserted ~~beach~~
rock strewn beach. Not a sight of life
or buildings besides the light house.
~~I~~ Choaked up with grief as I made
my way off shore leaving him behind.

46

W.P.H. 2012

What do I do now? Continue with
the crossing? Turn back and call it
a bust?
7-1-93   6:30 PM
Spent the last hour choked up with grief.
Can't go on without knowing John is ok.
Decided to find out, if I could, what's
on the other side of the island, so I motored
around it and found a small cove full
of rocks but out of the sea-way.
There's a large ramp made of timbers
for the launching and pulling of good sized
craft on the left, and straight on further
in, a small church-chapel painted white
and few cottages off to the right.
A few sheep here and there bleating their
favorite song.
 I took the other dinghy ashore (after setting
the anchor - a nice plow stored in the
forward chain locker in a spot which
looked safe), and pulled it up on the ramp,
I thought, a safe distance as the tide
was on the way out.
 The day was sunny and warm on this
side of the island . . . a glorious day.

What do I do now? Continue with
the crossing? Turn back and call it
a bust?

7-1-93   6:30 PM

Spent the last hour choaked up with greef.
Can't go on without knowing John is ok.
Decided to find out, if I could, whats
on the other side of the island so motered
around it and found a small cove full
of rocks but out of the sea-way.
There's a large ramp made of timbers
for the launching and pulling of good sized
craft on the left and straight on farther
in a small church chappel painted white
and with a few cottages off to the right.
A few sheep here and there bleating there
favorite song.
I took the other dingy ashore after setting
the anchor, a nice plow stored in the
forward chain locker, in a spot which
looked safe and pulled it up on the ramp
and thought a safe distance, as the tide
was on the way out.
The day was sunny and warm on this
side of the island a glorias day.

50

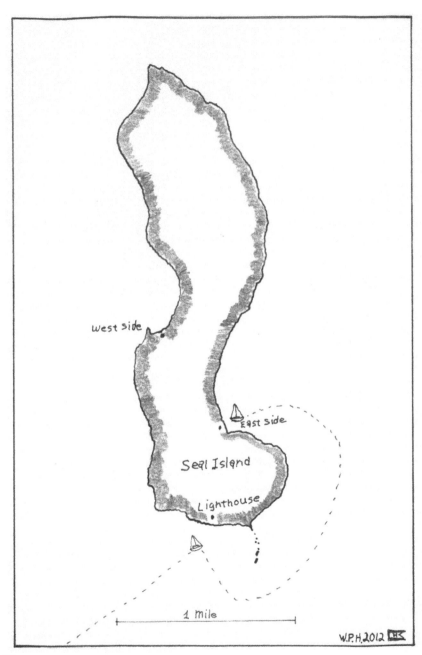

West side

East side

Seal Island

Lighthouse

1 mile

W.P.H. 2012

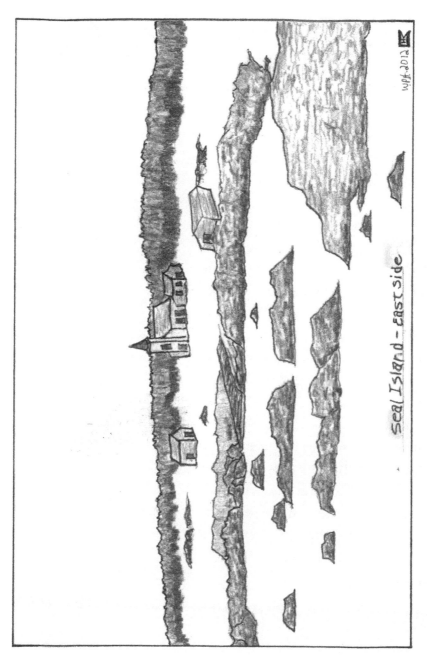

Seal Island - East side

7-1-93

Found some people near the first cottage
I came to. Two women were sitting on a bench,
and the one man was sawing some firewood
with a long, large-toothed handsaw.
I introduced myself, and told them about
how I had dropped my son off on the other
side of the island, and asked if there was
a way to get there without beating my way
through the thick undergrowth
of the nearby woods.
 Turns out there was a trail, which
turned out to be easy to find and easy
to follow. The island, as a guess, was about
half a mile wide at this point. And, about
halfway down the trail, there was John
headed in my direction. He couldn't believe
his eyes at seeing me. He was wet and
explained that his dinghy flipped in the
surf and threw him and his stuff out
in a second into the brine. After recovering
his stuff and the oars, he pulled the dinghy
up into the beach grass and left it upside
down there.
 Above the rocky beach
all he saw was a solid line of

7-1-93

I found some people near the first cottage I came to, two women were sitting on a bench and the one man was sawing some fire wood with a long, large toothed hand saw.

I introduced myself and told them about how I had dropped my son off on the other side of the island and asked if there was a way to get there without beating my way through the thick under growth off the near by woods.

Turns out there was a trail, which turned out to be easy to find and easy to follow. The island, as a guess, was about a mile wide at this point and about half way down the trail there was John headed in my direction. He couldn't believe his eyes at seeing me. He was wet and explained that his dingy flipped in the surf and threw him and his stuff out in a second into the brine. After recovering his stuff and the oars, he pulled the dingy up into the beach grass and left it up-side down there.

Above the rocky beach all he saw was a solid line of

54

wind-blown spruce, thick and impenetrable.
His first thoughts were of
bears and beasts, but then he thought
that there must be a trail somewhere to
service the lighthouse, and went about
to find it and get off the beach.
 After hearing his tale, and with him feeling
more secure about people and cottages not far
off, he agreed to help me find the dinghy
and carry it back to the cove so that
I would have it back on board as a spare.
 Not an easy task, mostly dragging it.
I am completely whooped.
After making sure John had enough money,
and feeling ok about leaving him in the
hands of a lobster fisherman, who said he
would put John up for a week until
he goes to the mainland to sell his
catch, buy supplies and bring John to
the bus station there, we exchanged farewells
and I headed back to the Kandahar.
I could't believe my good fortune. The
tide had gone out alright, about twelve
feet, and after dragging both dinghies down
the slippery weed-and-moss-covered ramp

wind blown spruce, thick and unpen-
-atrable and his first thoughts were of
bears and beasts but then he thought
that there must be a trail some where to
service the light house and went about
to find it and get off the beach.
After hearing his tale and he feeling more
secure about people and cottages not far
off he agreed to help me find the dingy
and carry it back to the cove so that
I would have it back on board as a spare.
Not an easy task, mostly dragging it and
I am compleatly wooped.
After making sure John had enough money
and feeling ok about leaving him in the
hands of a lobster fisherman who said he
would put John up for a week untill
he goes to the mainland to sell his
catch, buy supplies and bring John to
the bus station there, ~~and~~ exchanged farewells
~~and~~ I headed back to the Kandahar.
I couldn't believe my good fortune. The
tide had gone out alright, about twelve
feet, and after dragging both dingys down
the slipery weed and moss covered ramp

I made my way back to the Kandahar which
was now surrounded by huge weed and
moss covered rocks. Back on board about 6:30 PM.
Took a dip for a bath and to shake off the
exhaustion. The water was icy cold and
after clambering back on board to soap up
with lemon fresh Joy (it lathers in salt
water), it took a few deep breaths to
muster up the courage to jump back in
in order to rinse off.

7-1-1993   9:00 PM
In the cockpit contemplating what to do
next. I know I'm not getting underway tonight.
Feels good to be anchored, even among all of
these rocks.
 It's a bright evening, full moon in two days.
The sheep can be heard now and then as if
saying good night to one another. I bleat back
as the shadows overtake the island and the cold dampness
begins to settle in.

7-2   9:00 AM   Cape Sable, N.S.
Woke around 7:30 to a foggy morning. Quite
a contrast to the clear brightness of last night.

I made my way back to the Kandahar which was now surrounded by huge weed and moss covered rocks. Back on board about 6:30pm

Took a dip for a bath and to shake off the exhaustion, the water was icy cold and after clambering back on board to soap up with lemon fresh Joy (it lathers in salt water) it took a few deep breaths to muster up the courage to jump back in in order to rinse off.

7-1-1993   9:00pm
I'm the cockpit contemplating what to do next. I know I'm not getting under way tonight feels good to be anchored even amongst all of these rocks.

It's a bright evening, full moon in two days, the sheep can be heard now and then as if saying good night to one another I bleat back as the shadows overtake the island and the dampness begins to settle in.

7-2 9:00am. Cape Sable, N.S.
Woke around 7:30 to a foggy morning. Quite a contrast to the clear brightness of last nite.

I couldn't even see the boat ramp which
is only about a hundred yards off.
 My thoughts of getting an early start sank
like the tuna can I tossed overboard last
night. After relieving myself over the side
I crawled back in the port bunk for
another hour or so, then finally got up
from the sheer boredom of negative thoughts
and made some coffee.
9:00 PM 'Bout nine a breeze came up. The
fog cleared out pretty quickly, so I started
up the one banger, hoisted the main and
the anchor, and cleared the cove about nine
thirty. I had made up my mind to continue
on to Scotland alone no matter what.
The fresh breeze lifted my spirit, and there
was no stopping me. Once clear of the
rocky coast I shut down the engine,
pulled out the one-fifty genoa jib, and enjoyed
a five knot port reach for about three hours.
 Then the fun was over. The breeze
was gone as quickly as it came, and there I
was, sitting on a flat mill pond, surrounded
by fishing boats. The closest one about a
mile off, and a dozen more or so

I couldn't evan see the boat ramp which is only about a hundred yards off.

My thoughts of getting an early start sank like the tuna can I tossed over board last night. After relieving myself over the side I crawled back in the port bunk for another hour or so then finally got up from the sheer boardum of negative thoughts and made some coffee.

9:00 pm 'Bout nine a breeze came up and the fog cleared out pretty quickly so I started up the one banger, hoisled the main and the anchor and cleared the cove about nine thirty. I had made up my mind to continue on to Scotland alone no matter what. The fresh breeze lifted my spirit and there was no stopping me, once clear of the rocky coast I shut down the engine and pulled out the one fifty genoa jib and enjoyed a fine knot post reach for about three hours.

Then the fun was over, the breeze was gone as quickly as it came and there I was setting on a flat mill pond, surrounded by fishing boats. The closest one about a mile off and a dozen more or so

scattered farther off. I had watched them
all the afternoon, sitting shirtless in the
cockpit reading and enjoying the warmth of
the sun. Then about four o'clock I noticed
them all moving toward the mainland
as if someone had called them all home
for dinner.

 It was about dead calm then. Their exhaust
plumes hung in the air behind them as long
dark clouds, dirty and, in my mind, ugly
scars on the otherwise pristine scene.

 I contemplate following them in or remaining
out here for the night, and decide on going in.
Started up the engine and headed for the spot
that the fishing boats seem to be heading for.
Although I don't have a chart of the coast I
felt comfortable following other boats in.

 My speed though, of about five knots,
was only about half of the fishing boats.
In two hours time they had made the
eighteen or so miles and left me well
behind. I took a compass bearing of the
location where they all disappeared to and
searched with my binoculars for some sign
of a buoy. The land could be seen on the
horizon, stretching from my bow to distant starboard.

scatered further off. I had watched them
all the afternoon, sitting shirtless in the
cockpit reading and enjoying the warmth of
the sun. Then about four oclock I noticed
them all moving twords the mainland
as if someone had called them all home
for dinner.

It was about dead calm then and their exhaust
plumes hung in the air behind them as long
dark clouds, dirty and in my mind, ugly
scars on the otherwise pristene scene.

I contemplate following them in or remaining
out here for the night and decide on going in.
I started up the engine and headed for the spot
that the fishing boats seem to be heading for.
Although I don't have a chart of the coast I
feelt comfortable following other boats in.

My speed though of about five knots
was only about half of the fishing boats
and in two hours time they had made the
eighteen or so miles and left me well
behind. I took a compass bearing of the
location where they all disapeared to and
searched with my binoculars for some sign
of a bouy. the land can be seen on the
horizon streeching from my bow to distant starbord

62

In the last light of the setting sun I
spotted a red nun (buoy) and five minutes later
another. It was nearly dark as I entered
the narrow inlet protected by a breakwater
of large boulders.
 A small and cramped port
called Stoney Island Harbor was, in my mind, full
to capacity with eight or so forty-to-fifty
foot long-liners rafted together two
or three deep surrounding a sturdy main pier.
I'm told to tie up anywhere and chose
the port side of an old, green, wooden, long liner
with the name "Long Lines" spelled out
in black block lettering outlined with
white, across her stern.
Alton (Buzz) Smith, the captain of Stephanie Joy II, assisted
with the operation and invited me aboard
for a beer and a chat. During which time,
he gave me an old chart of the coastline
up to Liverpool, after I explained to him
how I happened to end up here for the night.
 The natives here are very friendly and the
language is the same as home on the Cape except
that after every sentence you simply add "eh".
As an example: Where ya from, "eh?"

In the last light of the setting sun I
spotted a red nun and five minutes later
another. It was nearly dark as I entered
the narrow inlet protected by a break-
-water of large ~~stones~~ boulders.

A ~~small~~ and ~~cramped~~ cramped port
called ~~Stoney Island~~ ~~Harbor~~ was, in my mind, full
to capasity with ~~thirty~~ or so ~~eight~~ forty to
fifty foot ~~long~~ liners rafted togeather two
or ~~three~~ deep ~~surounding~~ a sturdy main pier.
I'm told to tie up anywhere and ~~choose~~
the port side of an old, green, wooden, ~~long~~
-liner with the name "Long Lines" speled out
in ~~the~~ black, block, lettering out-lined with
white, across her stearn.
Alton (Buzz) Smith, the captain, ~~& Stephanie JyII~~ assisted
with the operation and invited me a-board
for a beer and a chat, during which time
he gave me an old chart of the coast line
up to Liverpool after I expained to him
how I happened to end up here for the night.
    The natives here are very friendly and the
language is the same as home on ~~the~~ Cape except
that after every sentence you simply add "a".
As an example: Where ya from, "a"?

"How long take ya from Cape Cod, eh?"
"Where ya goin', eh?" "By ya self, eh?"
I'm asked a lot of questions, and some of them
I'm still asking myself!
1 AM I mentioned a desire to walk to the nearest
store and was told it was 'bout five miles off "eh".
 So hitched a ride there and back with no trouble
at all. I was a little disappointed with the store
not having any "alkaline" double "A" batteries, but picked up
a twelve pack of Bud long necks to share with
whoever wanted one back on the pier.
 The double "A" batteries are for the G.P.S..
It takes nine of them. And, I've already gone
through the first nine in only five days, with
only using it seven times; only have nine
more fresh ones left. Am anxious to get
some sleep, but the long necks have lured
2 fishermen, brothers, to come onboard and tell stories
'till after 12:00. They had just come in from ten
days on the Grand Banks, hand-lining for
what ever was biting, and thankfully, mostly
Cod. My head is spinning after two beers,
a lot of emotion-commotion going round in my
head.

"How long take ya from Cape Cod, "a"?"
"Where ya goin', "a"? By ya self, "a"?"
I'm asked a lot of questions and some of them
I'm still asking myself!

1 AM I mentioned a desire to walk to the nearest
store and was told it was 'bout five mi. off "a".
So hitched a ride there and back with no trouble
at all but was a little disapointed with the store
not having any "double" "a" batteries but picked up
a twelve pack of Bud long necks to share with
who ever wanted one back on the pier.
The double "a" batteries ~~are~~ are for the G.P.S..
It takes nine of them and I've already gone
through the first nine in only five days with
~~only~~ only using it seven times, only have nine
more fresh ones left. I'm anxious to get
some sleep but the long necks have lured
2 fishermen Dontan to come on board and tell stories
till after 12:00they had just come in from ten
days on the "Grand Banks" hand lineing for
what ever was biteing and thankly mostly
Cod. My head is spinning after two beers,
a lot of emotion-comotion going round in my
head.

66

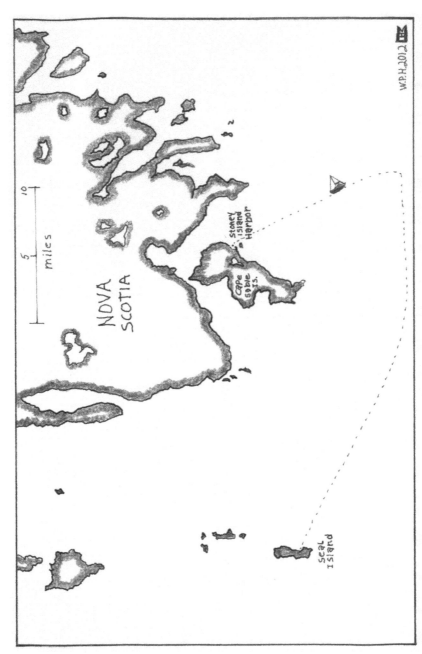

NOVA SCOTIA

miles
5   10

Stoney Island Harbor
Cape Sable Is.

Seal Island

W.P.H. 2012

67

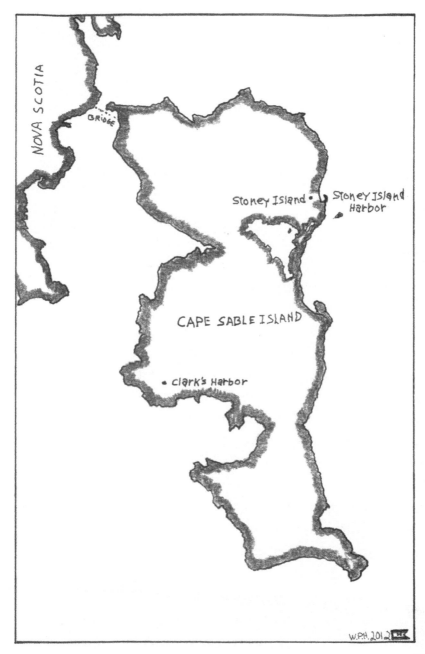

NOVA SCOTIA

BRIDGE

Stoney Island · ⸱ Stoney Island
Harbor

CAPE SABLE ISLAND

· Clark's Harbor

W.P.H. 2012

July 3, 1993   Six AM   Woke to a silence.
Most of the boats have gone out.
The ones left won't go today for some
reason or another. At 5:00 AM
it was a busy place. I decided to sit
tight and not be a part of the grand
exodus - went <u>back to sleep of a</u>
<u>throbbing head</u>. By the time breakfast
was finished with, and a resulting bowel
movement, a breeze came up and my
time to depart also.
Noon Before departing the harbor, I motored around
to the other side of the main dock where the
fuel pumps are located and topped off the
tank, .8 gal. Point 8 gallons, I was quite
embarrassed about the transaction, but now I
know how much fuel I have.
 Felt good to be heading out of the harbor.
I probably lost a day, considering now I feel
like I'm backtracking to resume my way.
 I didn't call anyone at home while in port.
No sense in worrying anyone there.

July 4, 1993   12 Noon
 Made about 100 miles since leaving

July 3, 1993 ~~6~~ six am. woke to a silence.
Most of the boats have gone out,
the ones left wont go today for some
reason or another. ~~From~~ at 5:00 ~~am to~~
it was a busy place I decided to sit
tite and not be a part of the grand
exodus, went back to sleep of a
throbing head. By the time breakfast
was finished with and a resulting bowel
movement a breeze came up and my
time to depart also.
noon Before departing the harbor I motered around
to the other side of the main dock where the
fuel pumps are located and topped off the
tank, .8 gal, point eight gallons, I was quite
embarrassed about the transaction but now I
know how much fuel I have.
Felt good to be heading out of the harbor
I probably lost a day considering now I feel
like I'm backtracking to resume ~~my way.~~
I didn't call anyone at home while in port,
no sense in worrying anyone there.

July 4, 1993 12:noon
Made about 100 miles since leaving

70

Stoney Island Harbor yesterday. As soon as I cleared
the harbor put up the main and set the jib
to about a 10 knot breeze, which steadily
increased to 20.
 It's blowing good now as I take a break
for lunch and a nap.

6 PM July 4, 1993
After lunch of coffee, lentil soup (Progresso)
from a can and bread with butter (real), I couldn't
close my eyes. Perhaps energy from the
storm. Exhausted now after bringing the
eight foot pram dinghy on board. Not a
good idea towing it behind - the waves
had filled it over the seats with water.
Pulling it over the rail took all the strength
I could muster. What a stupid stunt. Now
it's in the cockpit upside down (which is
the only way I could get it over the rail)
and half sticking up on the rail.
 I'm hove-to with the main at the third
reef-point which is as small as I can
set it, and the jib is rolled into a small
triangle. Both sails are backed

~~Stoney Island~~
~~harbor~~ harbor yesterday. As soon as I cleared
the harbor put up the main and set the jib
to about a 10 knot breeze which steadily
increased to 20.
It's blowing good now as I take a break
for lunch and a nap.

6 PM. July 4 1993
After lunch of coffee, lentil soup (Progresso)
from a can and bread with butter (real) couldn't
close my eyes. Perhaps energy from the
storm. Exhausted now after bringing the
eight foot pram dinghy on board. Not a
good idea towing it behind, the waves
had filled it over the seats with water.
Pulling it over the rail took all the strength
I could muster ~~What~~ a stupid stunt. Now
it's in the cockpit upside down (which is
the only way I could get it over the rail)
and half sticking up on ~~the~~ rail.
    I'm hove-to with the main at the third
reef point which is as small as I can
set it and the jib rolled in to a small
triangle both sails are backed

to starboard with the wind and waves
hitting the starboard side. My guess is
the wind about forty and the seas about
ten to fifteen feet and duration about
thirty or so. This is the worst storm
I've experienced with Kandahar, and she's
riding with no problem. Every now
and then a wave will slap the side and
throw spray over the dodger I'm under.
My position is 43:55 N 63:00 W or about
sixty miles off of Halifax, Nova Scotia.

July 5, 1993   44:1.3 N 61:3.2.W   8 PM
All night and all day the storm
is still blowing. The wind is out of the south
east more, and yesterday it was more out
of the south. After some more soup yesterday
evening and some rest, I reset the sails and
made a reach down east, C 056° mag. Made
about 60 miles. Need to make at least 100 mi. a day
in order to arrive in Scotland when Jim
MacDonald does. Gave myself 33 days to do it
and it's about 3 thousand miles. This is the end
of my seventh day.

to starboard with the wind and waves
hitting the starboard side. My guess is
the wind about forty and the seas about
ten to fifteen feet and duration about
thirty or so. This is the worst storm
I've experianced with Kandahar and she's
riding with no problem. Every now
and then a wave will slap the side and
throw spray over the dodger I'm under.
My position is 43:55 N 63:00 w or about
Sixty miles off of Halifax Nova Scotia.

July 5 1993   44:1.3 N 61:3.2 w   8:PM
All day and all night and all day the storm
is still blowing. The wind is out of the south
east more and yesterday it was more out
of the south. After somemore soup yesterday
evening and some rest I reset the sails and
made a reach down east, c 056 MAG. made about
60 miles. Need to make at least 100 mi a day
inorder to arrive in Scotland when Jim
McDonald does, gave myself 33 days to do it
and its about 3 thousand miles, this is the end
of my seventh day.

July 6, 1993   45:10N 60:3.3W   11AM
All night mostly starboard reach. Had
the wheel tied all night, kept jerking
myself awake. The wind came around
to mostly easterly and we're off course
to the north by about fifty mi. or so.
I see on the chart to the north is
Louisbourg Harbor about fifty miles off.
The genoa jib is beat up pretty badly;
needs more than I can do to be able to
continue on. Decided to head in and
find a sailmaker. Discouraging!

July 7   45:42N 60:15W   6:00AM
 I just finished scrambled eggs, toast,
coffee. Actually still on the coffee.
I'm in Fourchu (Fourchu), sounds
chinese but wherever, am glad to be
here. Yesterday set a course for Louisbourg,
and around six PM spotted a flashing
light. What a great feeling, but around
eight it was getting dark and at
the end of my wits. The shore line
was a couple miles off and nothing
but piles of rock and crashing
surf. I could see the light ok,

July 6, 1993   45:10 N 60:3.3 W   11 AM
All night mostly starboard reach had
the wheel tied all night kept jerking
myself awake. The wind came around
to mostly easterly and we're off course
to the north by about fifty mi or so.
I see on the chart to the north is
Louisburg Harbor about fifty mil. off,
the Genoa jib is beat up pretty badly
needs more than I can do to be able to
continue on, decided to head in and
find a sail maker. Discouraging!

July 7   45:42" 60:15 W   6:00AM
Just finished scrambled eggs, toast,
coffee. Actually still on the coffee.
I'm in Fourchu (FOUR CH U), sounds
chinese but where ever, am glad to be
here. Yesterday set a course for Louisburg
and around six pm spotted a flashing
light, what a great feeling but around
eight it was getting dark and at
the end of my wits. The shore line
was a couple miles off and nothing
but piles of rock and crashing
surf. I could see the light ok

76

but no sign of habitation any where
in sight. Just more rocks (big ones),
and crashing surf and beyond that
granite ledge outcroppings. I go
right to the light on a steel
framed tower about thirty feet high
and then, thank God an opening
in the hills of ledge and a buoy
off the port side. A long peninsula
to port running parallel to the
sea shore for a mile or so. And then
spotted off the port bow a pier, and then
another further on. As I got close by
the first pier, which was built out
of big logs criss-crossed and stacked
up like log cabin style, and filled in
with large rocks to make it solid,
and packed with gravel for the last
few feet above the high water line,
and a building of say 12 x16 on top of that,
and a pickup truck and someone waving
me to come near.
  I called over to him asking if I
could tie up for the night and got
a hearty "sure thing, eh" in reply.

but no sight of habitation any where
in sight, just more rocks (big ones),
and crashing surfe and beyond that
granite ledge out croppings. I go
right to the light on a steel
framed tower about thirty feet high
and then, thank God an opening
in the hills of ledge and a bouy
off the port side. A long peninseler
to port, rimming parralell to the
sea shore for a mile or so and then
spoted, of the port bow, a pier and then
another further on. As I got close by
the first pier which was built
of big logs I cris-crossed and stacked
up like log cabin style and filled in
with large rocks to make it solid
and packed with gravel for the last
few feet above the hi-water line
and a building of say 12 x 16 on that
and a pickup truck and someone waving
me to come near.

I called over to him asking if I
could tie up for the night and got
a hearty "sure thing a" in reply.

78

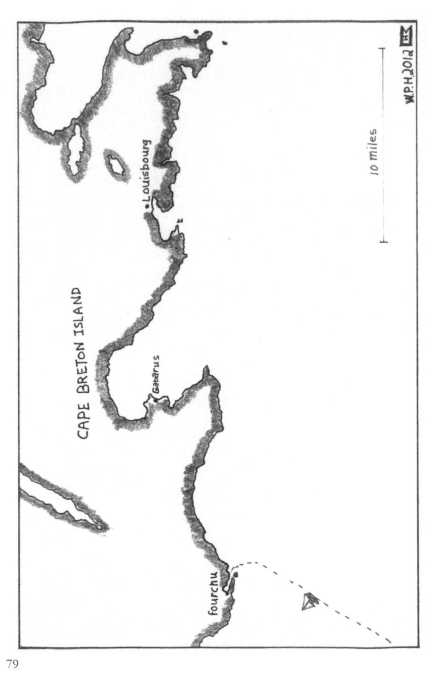

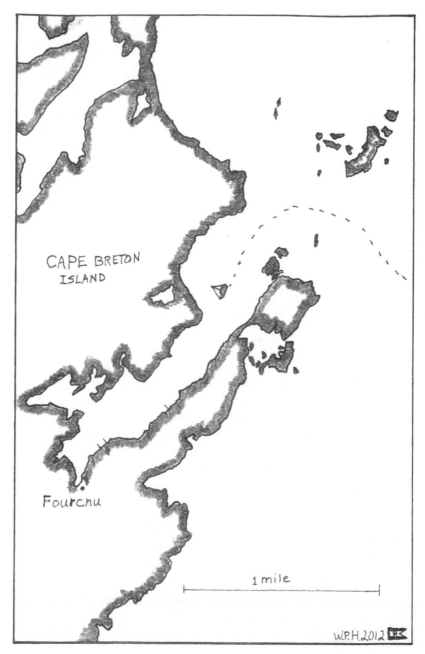

CAPE BRETON
ISLAND

Fourchu

1 mile

W.P.H. 2012

80

I saw three such piers: two on
this side of the harbor and one more
on the far side off in the distance.
There were four lobster boats;
three at piers and one on a mooring
in the center, about one hundred
yards off shore.
 I spotted four houses from where
I could see.
 A woman drove up as I was tying up to
a floating dock and came running over exclaiming
how she had been watching me for the
last two hours from a high point of
land and can't believe I sailed into Fourchu.
 "No one ever sails into here!" she said,
and wanted to know all about me. We talked
for a while the three of us, and she insisted
on me coming on over for something to
eat and people to meet. I hopped in her
car and we drove around the harbor
for about a half mile to a house; two
stories, with a brand new Lincoln parked
in the gravel drive. Inside was a phone
and three men; the owner and captain of
a boat (lobster), and the other two

I saw three such piers two on
this side of the harbor and one more
on the far side off in the distance.
There were four lobster boats
~~Three~~ at piers and one on a mooring
in the center, about one hundred
yards off shore.
I spotted four houses from where
I could see.
A woman drove up as I was tying up to
a floating dock and came running ~~over~~ exclaiming
~~how~~ she had been watching me for the
last two hours from a high point of
land and can't believe I sailed into Fourchu.
"No one ever sails into here" she said
and wanted to know all about me, we talked
for a while, the three of us and she insisted
on me comming on over for something to
eat and people to meet. I hoped in her
car and we drove around the harbor
for about a half mile to a house, two
stories, with a brand new lincoln parked
in the gravel drive. Inside was a stove
and three men. The owner and captin of
a boat, (lobster)   and ~~The~~ other two

were his crew for the season, which
lasts ten weeks, as I was told, and they
live here with him for the ten weeks.
They were all watching TV which didn't
come in all that great but the two crew
stayed and kept watching while the capt.
came out in the kitchen to find out about
me and to offer his assistance.
He offered me a ride into Sydney, which is
about one hour from here but probably
the only place to get my sail repaired.
"I'll take you in tomorrow" since the
weather is still too rough to check his
pots. I have some lobster chowder and
use his phone to call Margi.
 The sound of her voice turns me into
a puddle of goo. We just got back together
two weeks before I left - after fourteen
months of playing it cool,
cooling it down to get our bearings.
She says she will fly over to Scotland
when I arrive and help me to celebrate.
We leave it there and I ask her not to
call my family. John will be there in
a week or so to fill them all in,

were his crew for the season, which last ten weeks as I was told, and they live here with him for the ten weeks.

They were all watchen T.V. which didnt come in all that great but the two crew stayed and kept watchen while the capt. came out in the kitchen to find out about me and to offer his assistance. Sydney

He offered me a ride into ~~the~~ which is about ~~two~~ one ~~hours~~ from here but probaly the only place to get my sail repared. ~~and I~~ "I'll take you in tomorrow" since the weather is still to rough to chek his pots, and I have some ~~lobster~~ chowder and use his phone to call Margi.

The sound of her voice turns me into a puddle of goo. We just got ~~back togather~~ too ~~weeks~~ before I left. After ~~six~~ fourteen months ~~of either us~~ of playing it cool, coolin it down to get our bearings.

She says she will fly over to Scotland when I arrive and help me to celebrate.

We leave it there and I ask her not to call my family, John will be there in a week or so to fill them all in,

and they can all worry more then, when
they learn that John is not aboard
to save me, or perhaps they will all
worry less, knowing that. Either-way
ok.

Aboard; Fourchu, Cape Breton Island, NS
July 7, 1993   9 PM
Just returned from Sydney - thirty-five miles away, and <u>sooo</u> happy to be alive!
Malcolm MacDonald has a lead foot in his
new Lincoln Town Car. A long drive
through mostly wilderness, on two lane
roads, faster then I ever want to be driven
again. Got the sail repaired but not by
a sailmaker - none in town - not a sailmaker
to be found. Settled instead on a car
upholstery shop. Said he could do it right
away, but after seeing it, needed a few
hours. No Dacron available, had to
settle on a light brown rayon, but still darker
than light. We went and had lunch at a
diner while waiting. Roger Macleod, the guy
on the pier last evening, came along for
the ride, and between the two of them
I enjoyed the whole scene.

and they can all worry more then, when
they learn that John is not aboard
to save me or prehaps they will all
worry less, knowing that. Eather-way
OK,

Aboard; Fourchu, Cape Breton Island, N.S.
July 7, 1993   9:PM.   ~~Sydney - thirty-five miles away~~ to Halifax!
Just returned from ~~Sydney~~ and sooo happy!
Malcome McDonald had a lead foot in his
new Lincoln Town Car. A long drive
through mostly wilderness, on two lane
roads, faster then I ever want to be driven
again. Got the sail ~~required but won't by~~
a sailmaker - none in town - not a sailmake-
-er to be found. Settled instead on a car
upolstery shop, said he could do it right
away but after seeing it, needed a few ~~three~~
hours. No dacron ~~th~~ available had to
settle on a lite brown, ~~now~~ but still darker
than lite. We went and had lunch at a
dinner while waiting, Rodger McLeod, the guy
on the pier last evening came along for
the ride, and between the two of them
I enjoyed the whole scene.

86

July 8, 1993 Fourchu   9 PM

 A sunny day all day, no wind, hardly a
breeze. Roger's parents came by to visit
with him and they brought strawberries
and cream and butter and bread. And they invited
me to come over to his shack and share
in their bounty. While enjoying the strawberries
we noticed smoke coming out of the
lobster boat out on a mooring. Two men
were rowing as fast as they could towards the
pier - well one was rowing and the other was
waving his arms about and yelling in our
direction. Roger and I both put down
our strawberries and cream and ran towards
the pier to see what was going on. We heard
the plea for a fire extinguisher. I made
a dash for the Kandahar and grabbed two
of the five I was carrying on board and
dashed back just as their skiff reached
the pier. In another minute they were
heading back, jumping onto the lobster boat,
and each one using those extinguishers
and dowsing the fire with foam.
 Am ready to shove off in the morning.

July 8, 1993 Zourchu 9:PM
A sunny day all day no wind, hardly a
breeze. Rodgers parents came by to visit
with him and they brought strawberries
and cream and butter+Bread and they invited
me to come over to his shack and share
in their bounty. While enjoying the straw-
-berrys we noticed smoke comming out of the
lobster boat out on a mooring. Two men
were rowing as fast as they could twords the
pier - well one was rowing and the other was
waving his arms about and yelling in our
direction. Rodger and I both put down
our strawberrys and cream and ran twords
the pier to see what was going on. We heard
the plea for a fire extinguisher, I made
a dash for the Kondahar and grabed two
of the fire I was carrying on board and
dashed back just as their skiff reached
the pier, in another minute they were
heading back, jumping onto the lobster boat
and each one using those extinguishers
and dousing the fire with foam.
Am ready to shove off in the morning.

July 9, 1992   Fourchu, NS   10 AM
 Having another cup of coffee.
Malcolm & Roger came by early (around 7) and
brought me a chart of Southern Newfoundland,
well, the southern part of Avalon Pena, a
peninsula off of southern Newfoundland.
In particular, the fishing port of Trepassey
and the light of Cape Race. I don't plan
on stopping, but it's good to have a chart
of that area even though I plan on staying at
least fifty miles off as I skirt by this
last bit of land for two thousand miles of
open ocean. I've come about five hundred so
far and it's about three hundred and fifty more
to Cape Race. They also brought four nice
lobsters, all cooked up and in plastic bags. The
wind is supposed to come up this morning so
will be underway in a few. All set to go
but I feel the nervous anxiety creeping
in.

July 11, 1993 Louisbourg, NS   45:50 - 60:10 - 7 PM
 Arrived at the pier around 3 PM this afternoon.
What a stupid idiot. Left Fourchu two days ago,
and after motor sailing (with main) out of the harbor
a nice wind came up. Malcolm, Roger & Mariam

July 9, 1993 Fourchu, N.S. 10:AM
   Having another cup of coffee.
   Malcome & Rodger came by early (round 7) and
brought me a chart of southern Newfoundland,
well the southern part of Avalon Pena a
peninsular off of southern Newfoundland.
In particular the fishing port of Trepassee
and the light of Cape Race. I don't plan
on stopping but its good to have a chart
of that area even tho I plan on staying at
least fifty miles off as I skirt by this
last bit of land for two thousand miles of
open ocean. I've come about five hundred so
far and its about three hundred and fifty more
to Cape Race. They also brought four nice
lobster, all cooked up and in plastic bags. The
wind is supposed to come up this morning so
will be underway in a few. All set to go
but I feel the nerves any anxiety creeping
in.

July 10, 1993 Louisburg, N.S. 45.50.- - 60.10.- 7:PM
   Arrived at the pier around 3:PM this afternoon
What a stupid idiot. Left Fourchu two days ago
and after motor sailing (with main) out of the harbor
a nice wind came up. Malcome, Rodger & Marium

90

drove down to the last spit of land and
waved me off as I cleared the harbor
like in a movie. A nice northwest breeze
pushed me out of sight of land on a beautiful
beam reach.

❀

Down east we go a-sailing,
On a beautiful nor-west breeze,
Starboard rail on the downside,
Port wheel held tight with my knees.
I wave goodbye to New Scotland,
Old Scotland's where I'm bound,
To meet with a lass with more than my class,
And her voice the most beautiful sound.

❀

Well that's what it felt like then. After
six in the evening, the wind died. I ate and
stayed awake nearly all night but for a couple
of cat-naps in the cockpit. A bright
clear night, nearly a mill pond, could see a
light sweeping the horizon at regular intervals.
Thought it must be Louisbourg about thirty
miles off. In the morning I took a bearing
and headed for it. About 2 hours later around
six the fog set in. Just before noon I
came to rocky shore, large boulders
all around me, and then an eerie silence.

drove down to the last spit of land and
waved me off as I cleared the harbor
like in a movie. A nice northwest breeze
pushed me out of sight of land on a beautiful
beam reach.
Down east we go a-sailing, on a beautiful
nor-west breeze.
Starboard rail on the down side, port wheel
held tight with my knees.
I wave good bye to New Scotland, old Scotland's
where I'm bound,
To meet with a lass with more than my class
and her voice the most beautiful sound.
    Well that's what it felt like then. After
six in the evening, the wind died, I ate and
stayed awake nearly all night but for a couple
of cat-naps in the ~~the~~ cockpit. A bright
clear night, nearly a mill pond, could see a
light sweeping the horizon at regular intervals
thought it must be Louisburg about thirty
miles off. In the morning I took a bearing
and headed for it. About showers later around
six the fog set in. Just before noon I
come to a rocky shore, large boulders
all around me and then in eire silence,

The shore, thank God it was calm. The lighthouse
was right there some place, but couldn't
see it, hear it for damn sure. Didn't
know if the harbor was to the
right or to the left. Chose left and
picked myself around the rocks trying
to keep the shore in sight. Twenty feet
then twelve feet then back to twenty
feet. The depth sounder flashed and then
a buoy, then another, and soon I could make
out some sort of old fortifications on the
port side and then three boats, that looked
really weird like something out of the middle
ages, at anchor. I motored over to them and
dropped the hook in fifteen feet of water.
After backing down on the anchor to set it
a bit, killed the engine and just sat there
in awe. After lunch and a well deserved cup
of coffee, the fog lifted enough so I could
see the town farther in with buoys to
guide the way. At the main pier there were
some small fishing boats and a very large
old wooden ship like a galleon or something;
sort of a pirate looking ship. And the old
fort was magnificent, something you might

the shore, thank god its was calm, the light house was right there some place but couldn't see it, hear it for damn sure. Didn't know if the harbor was to the right or to the left. chose left and picked my self around the rocks trying to keep the shore in sight. twenty feet then twelve feet then back to twenty feet the depth sounder flashed and then a buoy, then another and soon I could make out some sort of old fortifacations on the port side and then three boats, that looked really weird like something out of the middle ages, at anchor. I motored over to them and dropped the hook in fifteen feet of water. After backing down on the anchor to set it a bit, killed the engine and just sat there in awe. After lunch and a well deserved cup of coffee, the fog lifted enough so I could see the town farther in with buoys to guide the way. At the main pier their were some small fishing boats and a very large old wooden ship like a galeon or something, sort of a pirate looking ship. And the old fort was magnificent, something you might

94

see in Europe. I picked up the hook and
putted into town. Arrived about three this
afternoon and tied up to a pier without any
skirting on it, just pilings encrusted with
marine growth, spaced about six to seven
feet apart. I am fortunate though to have
a ladder made of two by fours in order
to climb up to the top, which is about
fifteen feet from my deck. The ladder
is covered with slimy, weedy growth,
which I did my best to scrape off before
attempting to go ashore; at least some of it.
The town was hopping with activity.
Walt Disney Studios is in the process
of filming a movie here using the old
fort as a location. While wandering around
town came across a large storefront with
large windows and inside were a lot of sewing
machines, four or five women, and bolts
of material stacked about, but strangely no
business sign anywhere to be found. So I
wandered in and asked if it was possible
that they might have some white Dacron
thread, as I needed some aboard in case one
of my sails needed a little mending, and I had

see in Europe. I picked up the hook and
putted in to town. Arrived about three this
afternoon and tied up to a pier without any
skirting on it just pilings encrusted with
marine growth, spaced about six to seven
feet apart. I am fortunet though to have
a ladder made of two by fours in order
to climb up to the top which is about
fifteen feet from my deck. The ladder
is covered with slimmey, weedy growth,
which I did my best to scrape off before
attempting to go ashore, at least some of it.
The town was hopping with activity.
Walt Disney Studios is in the process
of filming a movie here using the old
fort as a location. While wandering around
town came accross a large store front with
large windows and inside were a lot of sewing
machines, four or five women and bolts
of material stacked about but strangely no
buisness sign anywhere to be found. So I
wandered in and asked if it was possible
that they might have some white Dacron
thread as I needed some aboard in case one
of my sails needed a little mending and I had

used all that I originally had brought with
me. Turns out it wasn't a store after all
but the wardrobe dept. for the film they
were shooting. And no they didn't have
any white Dacron, just eighteenth century
costumes hanging about and lying around, piled
on tables - fascinating - and busy. And they
asked if I knew how to sew. I did pick
up a spool of white rayon though, a gift from
the woman in charge.

Louisbourg, NS   July 12, 1993   8 PM
Spent the day roaming around town.
Woke to fog so thick couldn't see a hundred
feet. Cleared off by noon or earlier and
turned out a beautiful hot day. Well,
hot up here is eighty. T'was only
hot for a few hours though and the
rest of the day was perfect. Got a ride -
out to the lighthouse which is on a hill.
And what a beautiful overlook of the
harbor and the old fort here which is on
a peninsula jutting out to the north
and forming a natural breakwater protecting
the harbor and the fort which guards

with Wilson Evans

used all that I originally had bought with me. Turns out it wasn't a store after all but the wardrobe dept. for the film they were shooting ~~one~~ and no they didn't have any white Dacron just eighteenth century costumes hanging about and lying around, piled on tables — facinating — and busy and they asked if I knew how to sew? I did pick up a spool of white rayon though, a gift from the woman in charge.

Louisburg, N.S.   July 12, 1993 8, PM
Spent the day roaming around town.
Woke to fog so thick couldn't see a hundred feet, cleared off by noon or earlyer and turned out a beautifall hot day, well hot up here is eighty. It was only hot for a few hours though and the rest of the day was perfect. Got a ride — with Wilson Evans out to the lighthouse which is on a hill and what a beautiful overlook of the harbor and the old fort here which is on a peninsular jutting out to the north and forming a natural breakwater protecting the harbor and the fort which guards

98

the entrance to the St. Lawrence River and
the interior of the French claim of
Canada. Tomorrow's weather forecast is
for winds out of the north 10-15. I will
leave in the morning. Didn't really plan
on staying today but with the fog and
no wind, seemed safer here. Called Margi
this AM no answer. Called around 7:30 PM; talked for over an hour.
July 13, 1993   6:10 PM   46:02:63 58:54:21
 About seventy mi. off of Louisbourg.
Left this AM with a light breeze and no
fog. On a port reach all day making good
time until now. Wind is letting up and feel
the need to have a nap before dark. No
vessels in sight but I'm nearing the center
of the shipping channel and must be alert
all night.

7-14-93   6 AM   46:02:66   58:54:01
 Just took a LORAN reading and see that I have
made no headway at all since last night...bummed!
Started up the engine to charge batteries after having
the running lights on all night. Will motor for
awhile.

the entrance to the St Laurence River and the interior of the French claim of Canada. Tomorrows weather forcast is for winds out of the north 10-15 I will leave in the morning. Didn't really plan on staying today but with the fog and no wind, seemed saffer here. Called Margi this am. no answer. Called around 7:30 PM talked for over an hour.

July 13-1993   6:10 PM   46:02:63 58:54:21

About seventy mi off of Louesburg. Left this am. with a light breeze and no fog. On a point reach all day making good time untill now, wind is letting-up and feel the need to have a nap before dark, No vessels in sight but I'm nearing the center of the shipping channel and must be aleart all night

7-14-93   6 AM   46:02:66 58:54:01

Just took a loran reading and see that I have made no headway at all since last night.... bummed! started up the engine to charge batteries after having the running lights on all night will motor for a-while.

100

7-15-93 9 AM   46:06:38   57:53:18
 Motored for six hours till midnight. Then
a breeze came up and relief from the helm.
Starboard reach. Tied the wheel. Sat in cockpit
trying not to dose off. Get up now and then
to move around; pee, go below, get a snack,
put on more clothes under foul weather gear,
gets cold after midnight and damp.

7-15-93 4:30 PM   46:30:47   54:59:83
 Fog set in pretty thick before noon.
Motored, blowing. fog horn, nobody out here
but me, the idiot! Cold and wet. Handling
the lines with cold wet gloves on cold wet
hands with white skin that wants to peel
off. The seas are getting up a chop.

7-16-93 2:30 AM   46:05:08   54:11:24
Wind came up to a near gale; 30 at least,
and the seas to twenty. Came up fast out
of the north. Killed the engine about 9 PM and
backed the jib to a small triangle. It's blowing
me off to the southeast at a pretty good clip.
Tied off the wheel and spent most of the time
topsides under the dodger, keeping watch the
best I can, and trying to see through the

7.15.93 9:Am   46;06;38   57;53;18

Motored for six hours till midnight then
a breeze came up and relief from the helm.
Starbord reach, tied the wheel sat in cockpit
trying not to doze off. Get up now and then
to move around, pee, go below, get a snack,
put on more clothes under foul weather gear,
gets cold after midnight and damp.

7-15-93   4:30PM   46;30;47   54;59;83

Fog set in pretty thick before noon,
motored, blowing fog horn, nobody out here
but me, the idiot! Cold and wet, handeling
the lines with cold wet gloves on cold wet
hands with white skin that wants to peel
off. The seas are getting up a chop.

7.16-93 2:30Am   46;05;08 54;11;24

Wind came up to a near gale 30 at least
and the seas to twenty. came up fast out
of the north. Killed the engine about 9:pm and
backed the jib to a small triangle. Its blowing
me off to the southeast at a pretty good clip,
tied off the wheel and spent most of the time
topsides under the dodger keeping watch the
best I can and trying to see through the

beating rain. Came down below to make coffee. Quite a ride -

7-17   5:56 AM   46:12:60   54:07:88
All night, all day, half the next, last night
it blew, a good fifteen hours of hell.
Waiting in the cockpit for a ship to run
me over. Sitting in the bean bag chair I
brought along, dozing off with monotony
then coming to and jumping up to look
out for trouble. My jib is torn again.
Another seam let go, and the wind has frayed
the material for about three feet along the
unprotected edges. I'm about fifty miles
south of Trepassey, Newfoundland and decided
I must head in in that direction. Saw one
ship, a large freighter this morning at dawn
pretty close by, five or so miles off to the
south.

7-17   07:00   46:15:16   54:00:28
Took another reading to plot on the chart to see
if I'm heading in the right direction. Motoring
with main.

beating rain. Came down below to make
coffee, quite a ride —

7-17   5:50 AM   46:12-60   54:07:88
All night, all day, half the next, last night
it blew, a good fifteen hours of hell,
Waiting in the cockpit for a ship to run
me over. Sitting in the bean bag chair I
brought along, dozing off with monotony
then coming to and jumping up to look
out for trouble. My jib is torn again,
another seam let go and the wind has frayed
the material for about three feet along the
unprotected edges. Im about fifty miles
south of Trepassey, Newfoundland and decided
I must head in in that direction. Saw one
ship a large freighter this morning at dawn
pretty close by, five or so miles off to the
south.

7-17   07:00   46:15:16   54:00:28
Took another reading to plot on the chart to see
if Im heading in the right direction. Motoring
with main.

106

7-17   09:00   46:21:31   53:50:87
Still motoring with main sail. Wind has come
around out of the southeast, 10-15 about.
I can make out land on the horizon.

7-17   12:00   46:33:03   53:32:92
 High cliffs to my left off of port bow
about 10 mi. A lighthouse on most southern
point and another far off to starboard.
The one to starboard must be Cape Race.

7-17   2 PM   46:39:95   53:25:31
Red and white buoy with letters "ME"
painted on it. I see what looks like
a long jetty of piled up rocks further
on, 50° mag. Looks like a harbor entrance.
The cliffs here are magnificent. The land
rises abruptly up out of the sea, heavily
forested with misty clouds concealing
the upper most part. Waves crashing on
the rocky ledge at the base. Sea birds
large and small in the air all around,
and bobbing on the water all about me.
An eerie primeval setting and feeling.

7-17   09:00   46:21:31   53:50:87

Still motoring with mainsail, wind has come around out of the south east 10-15 about, I can make out land on the horizon

7-17   12:00   46:33:03   53:32:92

High cliffs to my left off of port bow about 10 mi. a light house on most southern point and another far off to starbord. the one to starbord must be Cape Race.

7-17   2:PM   46:39:95   53:25:31

Red and White buoy with letters "M E" painted on it. I see what looks like a long jetty of piled up rocks further on 50° mag. looks like a harbor entrance. The cliffs here are magnificent. The land rises abruptly up out of the sea, heavily forested with misty clouds concealing the upper most part, waves crashing on the rocky ledge at the base, sea birds large and small in the air all around and bobing on the water all about me. An erie primevel setting and feeling.

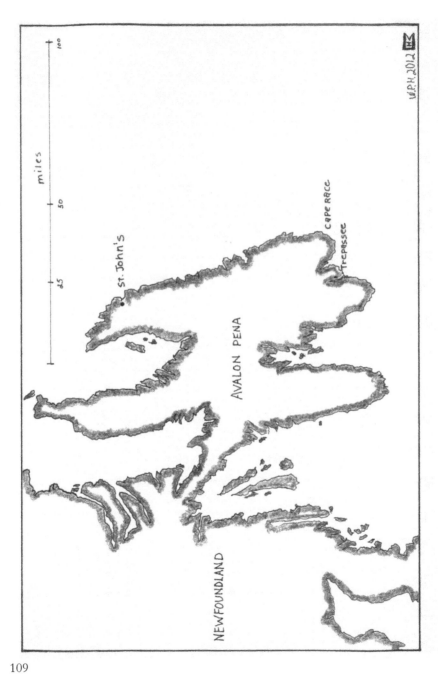

miles

25   50   100

St. John's

Cape Race
Trepassee

AVALON PENA

NEWFOUNDLAND

W.P.H. 2012

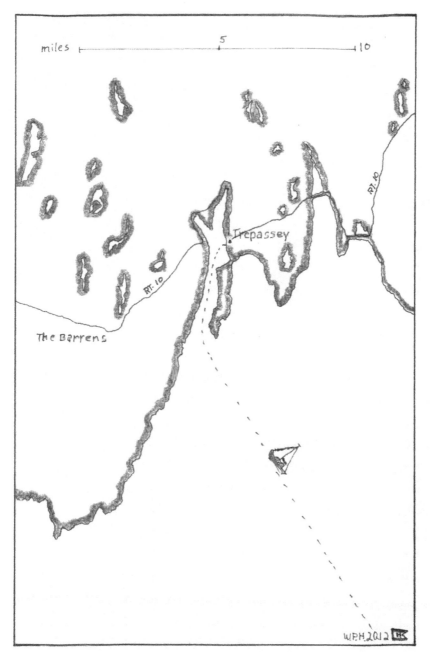

7-17   Trepassey Newfoundland   11 PM
 Arrived at the main pier here at three PM.
A wonderful harbor but I'm the only boat here.
A large commercial pier, must have been built
by the government. Lit up well with large
flood lights. Must have been built for
large fishing boats like the ones I saw
on the way in today, but the trouble is
they are all out of the water. Every one
lined up on the shore, on their keels,
braced well, seventy foot behemoths. All
trawlers, high and dry, a dozen of them.
 I was met by six or seven men on
the pier. Two pickup trucks. One car.
Friendly men, fishermen, curious about
me and helpful in every way. They wanted
to know if I had any cigarettes. Seems I could
have made a killing if I had brought a boat
load. They are expensive here. No I'm not a
smuggler I assured them, just a guy lost and
confused. I was glad to be here. I had enough
of the sea for a while. Inside I'm deflated.
Right now don't know what to do.
Called Margi 8 PM. No answer, tried again 10:30, no luck.
7-18   9:30 PM
 Last night turned in about midnight. At 2:30

7-17 Trepassey Newfoundland 11:PM

Arrived at the main pier here at three pm.
A wonderful harbor but I'm the only boat here.
A large comercial pier, must have been built
by the goverment. Lit up well with large
flood lights must have been built for
large fishing boats like the ones I saw
on the way in today but the trouble is
they are all out of the water every one
lined up on the shore, on their keels,
braced well, seventy foot behemiths, all
trawlers, high and dry, a dozen of them.
I was met by six or seven men on
the pier, two pickup trucks, one car.
Friendly men, fishermen, curious about
me and helpfull in every way. They wanted
to know if I had any cigarettes, seems I could
have made a killing if I had brought a boat
load, they are expensive here. No I'm not a
smuggler I assured them, just a guy lost and
confused. I was glad to be here, I had enough
of the sea for a while. Inside I'm deflated,
right now don't know what to do.
Called Margie 8 P.M. no answer, tried again 10:30, no luck.
7-18   9:30PM
Last night turned in about midnight, at 2:30

112

was startled awake by a lot of noise and
commotion. A large fishing boat came in
and tied up to the pier. Well, it really
backed up to the pier. It was about eighty
feet long, brimming with lights, and loud
diesel engines. The prop wash tossed me
around like a cork in a tempest. Good thing
·I was tied up good with long spring lines.
After tying up it left all its lights on, which
didn't make much sense to me seeing that the
pier was lit up like daylight, all night anyway, and it also left its engines running
the whole time it was there, which turned out
to be 'till this afternoon after it unloaded
its catch of crabs into a semi-trailer before
noon. Needless to say, didn't get much rest.
Mike Synyard, one of the fishermen I
had met yesterday on my arrival, came by
and invited me to a trout feast at his
house this afternoon and before that happened
a boy named Warren Perry came to the pier
riding his bicycle. Warren is about fourteen.
After talking with him a bit, I talked
him into going up the mast to retrieve a
jib up-haul I had lost during the
storm trying to haul up my working

was startled awake by a lot of noise and commotion. A large fishing boat came in and tied up to the pier, well it really backed up to the pier. It was about eighty feet long, brimming with lights and loud diesel engines. The prop wash tossed me around like a cork in a tempest, good thing I was tied up good with long spring lines. After tying up it left all its lights on, which didn't make much sense to me seeing that the pier was lit up like daylight all night anyway, and it also left its engines running the whole time it was there which turned out to be till this afternoon after it unloaded its catch of crabs into a semi trailer before noon. Needless to say didn't get much rest.

Mike Lynyard one of the fishermen I had met yesterday on my arrival came by and invited me to a trout feast at his house this afternoon and before that happened a boy named Warren Perry came to the pier riding his bicycle. Warren is about fourteen and after talking with him a bit I talked him into going up the mast to retrieve a jib up haul I had lost during the storm trying to haul up my working

114

jib. It had just slipped out of my fingers
when the bow came down into a wave and
at the moment my life seemed more important
then hanging on to the up-haul.
Anyway, Warren seemed delighted to be able
to be of assistance. After making him a
bosuns chair out of a spare piece of line, I
hooked him up to my main sheet up-haul
and cranked him up the mast, and brought
him back down with the jib up-haul in
his capable young hands.
  After the mission I asked what I could
do to pay him for his effort. He replied
that an American flag would be great, so
I gave him a five by seven of Old Glory,
which lit up his face like a Christmas tree.
  Later Mike Synyard came by, picked me up
and drove me to his house which was about
as big as a double wide mobile home, and feasted
me on as many fried trout and beers as I
could handle (a dozen trout, or so, and one beer).
  Seems as though every pond and puddle is
full of trout up here. I also found out
today that there's a daily mail run up
to St. John's where I would most likely
find a sailmaker.

jib. It had just slipped out of my fingers
when the bow came down into a wave and
at the moment my life seemed more important
than hanging on to the up haul.
Anyway Warren seemed delighted to be able
to be of assistance. After making him a
bosuns chair out of a spare piece of line I
hooked him up to my main sheet up haul
and cranked him up the mast and brought
him back down with the jib up haul in
his capable young hands.
After the mission I asked what I could
do to pay him for his effort and he replied
that an "american flag would be great, so"
I gave him a five by seven of old glory,
which lit up his face like a christmas tree.
Later Mike Jisnyard came by, picked me up
and drove me to his house which was about
as big as a double wide moble home and feasted
me on as many fried trout and beers as I
could handle (a dozen trout or so, and one beer).
Seems as though every pond and puddle is
full of trout up here. I also found out
today that there's a daily mail run up
to St. John's where I would most likely
~~find a sailmaker~~. find a sailmaker

116

7-19-93 Monday

Found a washing machine and dryer for
public use in the ground level basement of a
motel guests house. A nice place, with a restaurant
too, although I passed on that luxury. Seems
they have a little tourist trade here, mostly
sportsmen out for fishing and hunting.
The washer and dryer say $ .50 but won't start
until you put in $1.00.

 There's a drug store here, a branch bank, grocery,
post office, Royal Canadian Mounted Police station,
and a sub and pizza shop. The phone is in the pizza
shop, a wall-hung pay phone. I tried to call Margi
again yesterday morning at 10 AM but no luck.
Then again at 2 in the afternoon. Talked for
an hour and a half. Then at 9:30 last night
for fifteen minutes until someone in the
pizza shop needed to use the phone. But after
that, I called her right back and talked for
another hour. It might sound like l am doing
all the talking but it's a two-way street.
It's a catch-22 though. Mainly what this trip
is about is trying to get over Margi.

 Two years ago we began an affair. The most
wonderful affair I've ever known, having had
a few prior to her, actually being involved in

117

7-19-93 Monday

Found a washing machine and dryer for public use in the ground level basement of a motel gest house. A nice place, with a restaurant too, although I passed on that luxury. Seems they have a little tourist trade here, mostly sportsmen out for fishing and hunting.

The washer and dryer say .50 but won't start until you put in $1.00.

There's a drug store here, a branch bank, grocery, post office, Royal Canadian Mounted Police station, sub and pizza shop. The phone is in the pizza shop, a wall hung pay phone. I tried to call Marji again yesterday morning at 10:AM but no luck, then again at 2 in the afternoon, talked for an hour and a half, then at 9:30 last night for fifteen minutes untill some one in the pizza shop needed to use the phone but after that I called her right back and talked for another hour. It might sound like I am doing all the talking but its a two way street. Its a catch 22 though, mainly what this trip is about is trying to get over Marji.

Two years ago we began an affair. The most wonderful affair I've ever known, having had a few prior to her, actually being involved in

118

one when we began ours.
I fell so in love with her I couldn't sleep,
couldn't eat, couldn't do anything but think
about her and ways to be with her.
 I left the ten year relationship I was involved
with, gave up a new house I had just finished
building for myself and Sally, the woman
I was with, moved to a place of
my own and began freeing myself up for a new
life with (I hoped) Margi.
 She was doing the same thing, I thought.
Then eight months later, she dropped the bomb.
She told me she had begun seeing someone else.
 Ok, I was pissed. I called her a few names,
(choice ones). Wished later that I didn't, but
did, and apologized in a few days when my
blood pressure returned to normal and remorse
set in. (We only hurt the ones we love.)
 There it went, out the window, like so many
other plans and dreams in this life of magical
existence.
 For the next fourteen or so months we would
call each other once or twice a week, meet for
breakfast now and again trying to maintain
the friendship. I thought about her constantly

one when we began ours.

I fell so in love with her I couldn't sleep, couldn't eat, couldn't do anything but think about her and ways to be with her.

I left the ten year relationship I was involved with, gave up a new house I had just finished building for myself and Sally, the woman I was ~~involved~~ with, ~~I~~ moved to a place of my own and began freeing myself up for a new life with (I hoped) Margi.

She was doing the same thing, I thought, then eight months later, she ~~dropped~~ the bomb. she told me she had begun seeing someone else.

Ok I was pissed. I called her a few names, (choice ones) wished later that I didn't but did and appologized in a few days when my blood pressure returned to normal and remorse set in. (we only hurt the ones we love)

There it went, out the window, like so many other plans and dreams in this life of magical epistance

For the next fourteen or so months we would call each other once or twice a week, meet for breakfast now and again trying to maintain the friendship, I thought about her constantly

120

and my heart and guts were aching.
 I started therapy and joined a yoga group.
She joined the group a few weeks later, but
I found it very uncomfortable, and she joined
another group, which at the time seemed like a
good idea.
 I dated a few other women. She dated other men.
But my heart was always wondering about her.
 When Jim asked me if I wanted to go to Scotland
my heart seized upon the idea of getting away
from all the failures of the past, and changing
by breaking old patterns, an adventure
to find a new me.
 Laundry is finished, folded, and put into a sail
bag.

7-20-1993 8 PM

The ride to St. John's took about two hours
along a beautifully scenic road through a few
towns I would love to spend some time in.
 Just after passing a sign, "Welcome to St. John's",
we spotted a sign on a red barn "SAILMAKER".
Peter Helleran said he would have them repaired
in a day or two, to give him a call tomorrow.

and my heart and guts were acheing.

I started therapy and joined a yoga group
she joined the group a few weeks later but
I found it very uncomfortable and she joined
another group which at the time seemed like a
good idea.

I dated a few other women, she dated other men
but my heart was always wondering about her.

When Jim asked me if I wanted to go to Scotland
my heart seized upon the idea of getting away
from all the failures of the past and changeing
by way of breaking with old patterns, an adventure
to find a new me.

Laundry is finished, folded and put into a sail
bag

7-20-1993 8:PM

The ride to St. John took about two hours
along a beautifully scenic road through a few
towns I would love to spend some time in.

Just after passing a sign, welcome to St John's
we spotted a sign on a red barn "SAILMAKER".

Peter Helleran said he would have them repaired
in a day or two, to give him a call tomorrow

122

David White, the driver and I continued into
town so he could run his errands of picking
up parts and supplies for folks back in
Trepassey.
I was very surprised by St. John's. There's
pretty much anything you could want up there,
even an airport for jet planes. I
had no idea, way out here in the boondocks
of most eastern Canada. While here in Trepassey,
a barren, treeless area, looks like the end of
the world, with its large fish-processing plant
closed and abandoned, and what fisherman that are
left are on the government dole for two years so
they can figure out what to do next.
And me, also trying to figure out what
to do next. Do I continue on to Scotland or
turn around and head back to Margi? Think
I'll head up to the phone and call her.

7-2-1993   8PM
Cliff Nichol came by the pier this morning
and asked if I would like to take a ride
inland to see some caribou. I said yes, and
we took route 10 north around Shoal Point,
and then south and west out across the Barrens.

David White, the driver and I continued into town so he could run his errands of picking up parts and supplies for folks back in Trepassey.

I was very surprised by St John's, there's pretty much anything you could want up there even an airport for jet ~~planes~~ planes, I had no idea, way out here in the boondocks of most eastern Canada. While here in Trepassey, ~~the~~ a barren, treeless area, looks like the end of the world with its large fish processing plant closed and abandoned and what fishermen that are left on the government doll for two years so they can figure out what to do next.

And me, I also trying to figure out what to do next. Do I continue on to Scotland or turn around and head back to Margi? I think I'll head up to the phone and call her.

7-21-1993   8:PM
Cliff Nichol came by the pier this morning and asked if I would like to take a ride inland to see some caribou. I said yes and we took route ten north around Shoal Point and then south and west out accross the Barrens

124

Once on the Barrens, as it's called, it didn't
take long to spot a herd to our right
about two or three miles off in the distance
and good luck they were moving in our
direction so Cliff pulled over and parked his
Mustang and in ten or fifteen minutes the
whole herd of a few hundred, I guessed, crossed
the road in front of us close enough to
smell them.
  Got back to the pier in plenty of time to
call the sailmaker, Peter Helleran, who said
I can pick them up tomorrow anytime. They're
all set. Bought some ground beef at the
market and celebrated the day with a hamburger.
I'm pretty much a vegetarian and have been for
a few years, but feel a real craving for a hamburger
once in a while. Baked a nice potato, and with
lettuce, tomato and onion on the burger - - - a
feast. Don't get me wrong, I love beans and rice.
Also called David White and asked if I could go
to St. John's with him in the morning. He
said he'd pick me up at the pier around six.
Feeling restless, going for a walk.

Once on the Barrens, as its called, it didnt take long to spot a heard to our right about two or three miles off in the distance and good luck they were moving in our direction so Cliff pulled over and parked his mustang and in ten or fifteen minutes the whole heard of a few hundred, I guessed, crossed the road in front of us close enough to smell them.

Got back to the pier in plenty of time to call the sailmaker Peter Helleren who said I can pick them up tomorrow anytime their all set. Bought some ground beef at the market and celebrated the day with a hamburger. Im pretty much a vegetarian and have been for a few years but feel a real craving for a hamburger once in a while. Baked a nice potato and with lettuce, tomato and onion on the burger --- a feast. Dont get me wrong I love beans and rice.

Also called David White and asked if I could go to St. John's with him in the morning and he said he'd pick me up at the pier around six. Feeling restless going for a walk.

7-22-1993 10:30 PM
Just got off the phone with Margi. Told her
of my plan to continue on to Scotland.
An hour an a half, the time goes by so fast
when talking with her, and I feel close. She
feels close. But, walking out of the little shop
where the pay phone is and along down the dark,
damp road to the pier, I felt so far away and
alone. This trip has brought us closer together,
at least the idea of it. As soon as I mentioned
the idea of it to her, she moved in closer to me.
It's what I wanted and hoped for for a year and
more. Now I hope she'll be there on my return.
She said when I get to Scotland to give her a
call and she will fly over to be with me and
celebrate. Now all I have to do is get there.
Picked up the sails today. It took all
of the cash I had left, except for fifty dollars.
Three hundred and fifty to take out the auto
upholstery (brown), which I paid two-hundred
for back in Nova Scotia. It was replaced with
Dacron and re-stitched; and re-stitched the working
jib also. Stopped by the R.C.M.P. station and
informed them of my plan to make the crossing
and filed a float plan. Time for bed.

7-22-1993   10:30 P.M.

Just got off the phone with Margi, told her of my plan to continue on to Scotland.
An hour and a half, the time grew by so fast when talking with her and I feel close, she feels close. But walking out of the little shop where the payphone is and along down the dark damp road to the pier I felt so far away and alone. This trip has brought us closer togeather at least the idea of it. As soon as I mentioned the idea of it to her she moved in closer to me. It's what I wanted and hoped for for a year and more. Now I hope she'll be there on my return. She said when I got to Scotland to give her a call and she will fly over to be with me and celebrate. Now all I have to do is get there.
    Picked up the sails today and it took all of the cash I had left except for fifty dollars. Three hundred and fifty to take out the auto upholstery (brown) which I paid two hundred for back in Nova Scocia and replace with dacron and restitch, and restich the working jib also. Stopped by the R.C.M.P. station and informed them of my plan to make the crossing and filed a float plan. time for bed.

7-23-1993 Trepassey N'fld. noon.

What would frighten me the most,
To sail my boat off the coast,
Vanish in the endless sea,
Never more my love to see,
Friends and loving family.

Or stay and make my daily bread,
One day to lay my weary head,
Beneath the roots of yon stately tree,
Never more the sea to see.

I choose today to sail away,
Let go of those held dear,
See each moment's joy,
Not each moment's fear.

It matters not where I lay,
Under sea or tree,
But only as I love,
And only if my love is free.

Spent the morning hanking the genoa jib
and stowing away stuff that I have been using

2-23-1993 Trepassey N'fld. noon.

What would frighten me the most,
To sail my boat off the coast,
Vanish in the endless sea,
Never more my love to see,
Friends and loving family.

Or stay and make my daily bread,
One day to lay my weary head,
Beneath the roots of yon statley tree,
Never more the sea to see.

I choose today to sail away,
Let go of those held dear,
See each moments joy,
Not each moments fear.

It matters not where I lay,
Under sea or tree,
But only as I love,
And only if my love is free.

Spent the morning hanking on the genoa jib
and stowing away stuff that I have been using

while here at the pier. Cooked up a big
pot of rice, went to the store and bought
some fresh veggies and blanched them so to
have a few days of food prepared. No refrigeration.
A few bags of ice will keep the milk for my
tea and oatmeal fresh for a while.
Lots of feelings going on in the gut. Go to
Scotland? Go back home??
Foggy, dreary, damp this morning, I've been
hesitating, procrastinating, hoping for a wind,
a breeze. Weather report from the store keeper -
ten to fifteen out of the southwest but a
southwest wind here brings more moisture
which condenses over the cold sea water
and causes fog. Not a breeze yet. Just
dreary!

7-24-1993   9:30 AM   46:46:29   52:42:42
Making coffee. No wind. Whales right next
to me, four or five. I mean right next
to me, can smell their bad breath every time
they blow. They are heading north. It's raining.
I started up the one banger as soon as I
heard the first one in order to let them

while here at the pier. Cooked up a big pot of rice, went to the store and bought some fresh vegies and blanched them so to have a few days of food prepared, no refrigeration, a few bags of ice will keep the milk for my tea and oatmeal fresh for awhile.

Lots of feelings going on in the gut. Go to Scotland? go back home??

Foggy, dreary, damp this morning, I've been hesitating, procrastinating, hoping for a wind a breeze, weather report from the store keeper, ten to fifteen out of the south west but a south west wind here brings more moisture which condenses around the cold sea water and causes fog. Not a breeze yet just dreary!

2-24-1993   9:30 AM   46°46′.29 52°42′.42
Making coffee. No wind, whales right next to me, four or five, I mean right next to me, can smell their bad breath every time they blow. They are heading north, its raining I started up the one banger as soon as I heard the first one in order to let them

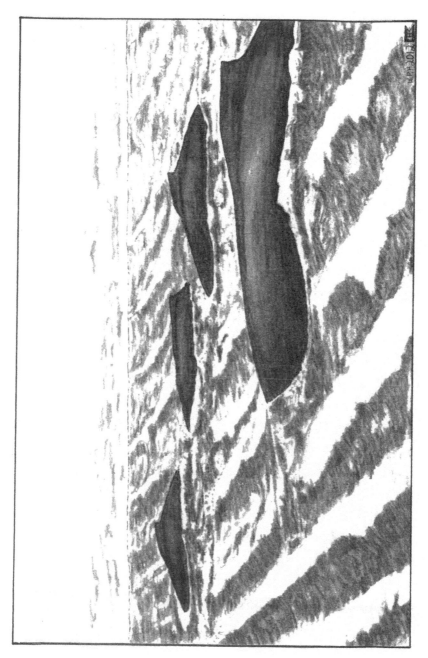

know I'm no threat. At least that's the
way I heard it (if you see whales, make noise
so they know you're not another whale that
might want to fight for the females).
I need to charge the batteries also and make
some headway.
 Left Trepassey yesterday about four o'clock in
the afternoon. A breeze did come up and the
fog lifted enough to see my way out and
clear the harbor. Felt good to be underway.
All the jitters cleared from me once I untied
the last line holding me to the pier. Once
I let go, the energy (my energy) shifted,
new thought patterns took over.
 The wind held up until I cleared Cape
Race and set course for the northern
tip of Ireland: 80°, 1738 NM to the
Bloody Foreland. That's what it says on the
chart, chart number 121 North Atlantic Ocean
Northern Sheet. I've come about 1262 mi. so far.
Last night when I was about fifty miles off
the coast the wind died. Around 2:30 AM
decided to have a nap in the cockpit. Woke about
4:30 AM. Still no wind. Relieved myself over the
side. Pretty calm, no problem.

know I'm no threat, at least that's the way I heard it (if you see whales, make noise so they know your not another whale that might want to fight for the females). I need to charge the batteries also and make some headway.

Left Trepassey yesterday about four oclock in the afternoon. A breeze did come up and the fog lifted enough to see my way out and clear the harbor. Felt good to be underway, all the jitters cleared from me once I untied the last line holding me to the pier. Once I let go, the energy (my energy) shifted, new thought paterns took over.

The wind held up until I cleared Cape Race and set course for the northern tip of Ireland 80°, 1738 N.M. to the Bloody Foreland, that's what it says on the chart, chart number 121 NORTH ATLANTIC OCEAN NORTHERN SHEET. I've come about 1262 mi so far. Last night when I was about fifty miles off the coast the wind died. Around 2:30 am decided to have a nap in the cockpit. Woke about 4:30 am still no wind relieved myself over the side, pretty calm no problem.

136

Whales are gone. Once I started the engine
they moved away to the north. What an
awesome sight, goose bumps. Finished coffee,
corn muffin with almond butter and banana.

7-24   1:30 PM   46:55:00   52:28.49   1703 NM
To Bloody Foreland Way Point #4
Wind picked up this AM. Fog & rain cleared out for
a few hours. Saw a large freighter to my
north about five miles heading for St. John's.
Too close for comfort. One of those guys could
run me over and never know it. I have
a nervousness in my gut.

7-24   5:20 PM   47:02.84 52:20.46 W.P. #4 1694 NM
Five to ten out of the south west, right on my
back. Starboard reach. Off course but I'm moving
some at least.

7-25   6:30 AM 47:13.37 51:53.18 #4 1673 NM
Drifted all night. No wind. Not a breath.
Nervous cat naps in the cockpit.

                                    Course 81°
7-25   7 PM   47:39.43 50:51.46 WP #4   1623 NM
Really rough. Seas & wind increased all day.

Whales are gone once I started the engine
they moved away to the north. What an
awsome sight, goose bumps. Finished coffee,
corn muffin with almond butter and banana.

7-24 1:30 PM   46:53:00   52:28:49   1703 N.M
TO BLOODY FORELAND WAYPOINT # 4
Wind picked up this aa, fog & rain cleared out for
a few hours, saw a large frieghter to my
north about five miles heading for St. John's.
To close for comfort, one of those guys could
run me over and never know it. I have
a nervousness in my gut.

7-24 5:20 PM   47:02.84 52:20.46   W.P.#4 1694 N.M
Five to ten out of the sou-west right on my
back. Starboard reach, off course but I'm moving
some at least.

7-25   6:30 AM   47:13.37   51:53.15   #4 1673 N.M.
Drifted all night. No wind, not a breath.
Nervous cat naps in the cockpit.

7-25 2:PM 47:39.43 50:57.46 W.P.#4 Course 81° 1603 N.M.
Really rough. Seas & wind increased all day

138

Blowing 25-30, seas 8-18 flying genoa only, on
port reach. Moving right along. Wind out of the
north. Around noon a two-engine plane buzzed
me. Came from behind me at near wave top
level. Two men in the cockpit up front.
The whole fuselage was slung under the wings
and the engines too. They went by at about
two hundred and fifty miles an hour and
close enough for eye contact. They
made a sweeping right hand turn and
headed back the way they came. No military
markings but looked like a government aircraft.
I figure they picked me up on radar and came
by to check me out.

Course 82°

7-26-1993 6PM   48:27.38 48:25.85 WP #4 1515NM
Still blowing pretty good, 25-30, reaching with
genoa only. Buzzed again by same plane
that buzzed me yesterday. Came by so close I
could see the pilots teeth as he smiled and
waved. What a rush. He had to tilt his left
wing up in order not to hit my mast.
Did about 125. mi. since yesterday at the same
time of day. About 190 mi. off of St. John's.

Blowing 2530, seas 8-18 flying genoa only, on port reach, moving right along, wind out of the north. Around noon a two engine plane buzzed me. Came from behind me at near wave top level. Two men in the cockpit up front and the whole fuselage was slung under the wings and the engines too. They went by at about two hundred and fifty miles an hour and close enough for eye contact. ~~Made~~ They made a sweeping right hand turn and headed back the way they came. No military markings but looked like a government aircraft. I figure they picked me up on radar and came by to check me out.

7 Dec 1993 6:PM   48:27.38 48:25.85 WP.#4/515 NM. counsel 82°
Still blowing pretty good 25-30 reaching with genoa only. Buzzed again by same plane that buzzed me yesterday, came by so close could see the pilots teeth as he smiled and waved. What a rush, he had to tilt his left wing up inorder not to hit my mast.
Did about 125 mi. since yesterday at the same time of day. About 190 mi. off of St. Johns

140

7-27-1993   06:00 AM   48:52.09   47:06.87 #4 1458
Wind out of the north 5-10. Seas have calmed
down quite a bit. Cold, damp, no sun. Overcast
is high and dark like a storm passing overhead.
It's bright on the horizon way off all around.
Winds are beginning to shift from north to more
easterly. Will put up the mainsail after breakfast.

7-27   6PM   49:08.9   46:04.23   WP#4 1413
Did almost a hundred miles since yesterday.
Winds have decreased steadily all day and have come
around now out of the south. The seas are
coming from three directions at once. The
bigger ones from the north, smaller ones from
the east, and smaller ones yet coming from
the south. My course, 83° magnetic, which is
about 65° true, east-northeast. Have been tacking
to the north with genoa and main, and have slowly,
during the afternoon, come back to my
rhumb line, which is a pencil line I drew on the
chart from Cape Race N fld. to the Isle of Islay,
off of the Scottish west coast. I'm well north of the
line, about seventy miles or so. What I meant to say
is, I slowly came back to my course, which is
now 83° magnetic according to what the GPS is
telling me.

7-27-1993 06:00 AM   48:52.09 4706.87 #4 1458
Wind out of the north 5-10, seas have calmed
down quite a bit, cold, damp, no sun, overcast
is high and dark like a storm passing over head,
its bright on the horizon way off all around.
winds are begining to shift from north to more
easterly, will put up the main sail after breakfast.

7-27 6:PM   49:08.95 46:04.23 W.P.#4 1413
Did almost a hundred miles since yesterday.
Winds have decreased steadaly all day and have come
around now out of the south. The seas are
comming from three directions at once. The
bigger ones from the north smaller ones from
the east and smaller ones yet comming from
the south. My course 83° magnetic wich is
about 45° true eastnortheast. Have been tacking
to the north with genoa and main and have
slowly during the afternoon come back to my
rube line which is a pencil line I drew on the
chart from Cape Race N'fld. to the isle of Islay.
off of the Scottish west coast. I'm well north of the
line, about seventy miles or so, what I went to say
is I slowly came back to my course which is
now 83° magnetic acording to what the G.P.S. is
telling me.

142

7-28   10 AM   49:09.02   45:44.58   WP#4 1402 NM
No wind for the last fourteen hours.
Put new batteries in GPS. They last about two and a
half hours. Sometimes takes twenty min. to get
a reading. Works best when it's calm and I
hold it over my head. Slept in the cockpit
off and on since midnight while sitting in the
bean bag chair I brought along. Pretty tired.
Drifted all night with sails flapping. Only made
about ten miles all night. Wind starting to pick up
just a little out of southwest.

7-28   5:30 PM   49:26.84   45:00.14   #4 1368NM C 84°
Have been running downwind all day. Sails
wing on wing. Set spinnaker pole on genoa
to starboard and tied back main boom to
port. On the wheel for the last eight hours
trying to keep her on a straight course. Hard
work. My shoulders are aching. All that work
for thirty miles.

7-29   6 AM   50:07.76   44:42.42   #4 1339 C 86°
Thirty miles last twelve hours. Wind has been
steadily increasing all night out of the southwest.
Now blowing twenty to thirty. Seas rough, 10-15.

7-28 10:AM   49:09.02 45:44.58 WP#4 1402NM.

No wind for the last fourteen hours.
Put new batteries in G.P.S. they last about two and a
half hours, sometimes takes twenty min. to get
a reading, works best when its calm and I
hold it over my head. Slept in the cockpit
off and on since midnight while sitting in the
bean bag chair I brought along. Pretty tired
drifted all night with sails flapping only made
about ten miles all night. Wind starting to pick up
just a little out of southwest.

7-28 5:30PM   49:26.84 45:00.14 #4 1368NM C.84°

Have been running down wind all day sails
wing on wing. Set spinnaker pole on genoa
to starboard and tied back main boom to
port. On the wheel for the last eight hours
trying to keep her on a straight course, hard
work, my shoulders are acheing. All that work
for thirty miles

7-29 6:AM   50:07.76 44:42.42 #4 1339 < 86°

Thirty miles last twelve hours wind has been
steadaly increasing all night out of the south west
now blowing twenty to thirty seas rough 10-15.

144

Last night before dark hauled down the main
and backed the jib, and hove to for some rest.
Went down below and stretched out on the port
side settee/bunk for some shut eye. Slept like a
log until midnight. Crossed the 50th parallel.
After midnight made some coffee. Filled large thermos
and flew the genoa on a northeast reach, a fast
one through the fog. Haven't mentioned it yet
but the birds out here are amazing. I swear
the same ten or so have been staying with me
ever since I left Cape Race. When it's windy
they fly about gliding and soaring all around me
and when it's calm they mostly sit and bob about
all around me paddling to keep up. Sometimes
coming in pretty close, ten feet or so, and give me
the eye. They are good company and I don't feed
them, just talk, ask them questions and tell them
what I'm doing. For the first few days there
were some puffins also, but they are gone and
the ones now are quite large, like a large gull,
but not gulls as I know them. These are pretty
quiet, mostly white with some grey.

7-29   2:30 PM   50:02.13 43:46.86   #4 1309 C 85°
Stopped for lunch, hove to. That means I've flattened

Last night before dark hauled down the main and backed the jib and hove to for some rest. Went down below and stretched out on the port side settie/bunk for some shut eye. Slept like a log untill midnight crossed the 50th parralel. After midnight made some coffee filled large thermous and flew the genoa on a northeast reach, a fast one through the fog. Haven't mentioned it yet but the birds out here are amazing. I swear the same ten or so have been staying with me ever since I left Cape Race. When its windy they fly about gliding and soaring all around me and when it's calm they mostly sit and bob about all around me paddeling to keep up. Some times comming in pretty close, ten feet or so, and give me the eye. They are good company and I don't feed them, just talk, ask them questions and tell them what I'm doing. For the first few days there were some puffins also but they are gone and the ones now are quite large like a large gull but not gulls as I know them these are pretty quiet, mostly white with some grey.

7-29 2:30 PM 50:02.13 43:40.810   #4 130 c 85°
Stopped for lunch, hove to, that means die flattened

out the sails, or in this case with only the jib
flying. I've headed into the wind long enough to
roll it up part way, tie it off amidships so
it's flat, and then turned the rudder so I'm broadside
to the wind. I'm still making some headway
along the troughs and the sail keeps me from
rolling side to side. The wind is coming over
the starboard rail, and the waves are slapping
the freeboard to starboard. But I'm dry thanks
to the weather canvas cloths I put over the railings.
Today Jim arrives in Glasgow, and I'm
not anyway going to make it there this week
or next the way things are going. Six days
out and not quite one quarter of the way there.
I lost about a foot of seam on the genoa.
Will need to take it down and try to sew it
up myself, but it's too rough to attempt right
now. Thirty-two days out of Plymouth. With
good sails I'd be there by now. Big learning
curve! Saw jet contrails heading east. Thought of Jim.
7-29 7 PM   50:00.58   43:29.76   #4 1300 NM C 85°
Sixty eight mi. since yesterday evening, not good.
Seas are really rough, twenty to thirty foot, some
more. About sixty feet apart. Lots of wind blown
white caps. Nothing to do but keep plugging
along.

151

out the sails or in this case with only the jib
flying, dive headed into the wind long enough to
roll it up part way and tie it off amidships so
its flat and then turn the rudder so I'm broad
side to the wind. I'm still making some headway
along the troughs and the sail keeps me from
rolling side to side. The wind is comming over
the starboard sail and the waves are slapping
the freeboard to starboard but I'm dry thanks
to the weather canvis cloths I put over the railings.

Today Jim arrives in Glasgow and I'm
not anyway going to make it there this week,
or next the way things are going. Six days
out and not quite one quarter of the way there.
I lost about a foot of seam on the genoa.
Will need to take it down and try to sew it
up myself but its to rough to attempt right
now. Thirty two days out of Plymouth, with
good sails I'd be there by now, big learning
curve! Saw Jet contrails heading east, thought of Jim

7-29 7:PM   50.00,58 43:29.76 #4 1300 NM °85°

fifty eight mi. since yesterday evening, not good.
Seas are really rough twenty to thirty foot, some
more, about sixty feet apart. Lots of wind blown
white caps nothing to do but keep plugging
along.

Have the genoa rolled up with only six
or seven feet sticking out. And have the
line tight amid-ships and the wheel tied
off with a little starboard weather helm, so
the waves hit me on the starboard stern
quarter. I'm moving right along towards the
east at about five knots. It's a comfortable ride
with me under the dodger, on the port side in
the bean bag chair.

7-30 10 AM   49:52.00 42:23.18 WP#4 1266 C 84°
Moved right along all night. The wind and
seas diminished gradually over the last fifteen
hours. Put up the mainsail around daybreak
and let out the genoa all the way. Am on a
starboard reach, been in the cockpit all night
cat napping. Large school of dolphins went by
me about an hour ago, like I was standing still.
They were all around me. Some came pretty close
and looked me in the eye. Great company.

7-30-93 7 PM   50:07.61 41:56.01 WP#4 1244 NM
Winds have died down to nothing. Amazing how
fast the seas get calm after the wind dies down.
Will need to turn on the running lights tonight.

Have the genoa rolled up with only six
or seven feet sticking out and have the
line tight amid ships and the wheel tied
off with a little starboard weather helm so
the waves hit me on the starboard steam
quarter. I'm moving right along towards the
east at about five knots. It's a comfortable ride
with me under the dodger on the port side in
the bean bag chair

7-30 10:AM   49:52.00   42:23.18   WP: #4 1266   C 84°
    Moved right along all night. the wind and
seas diminished gradually over the last fifteen
hours. Put up the mainsail around daybreak
and let out the genoa all the way. Am on a
starboard reach, been in the cockpit all night
cat napping. Large school of dolphins went by
me about an hour ago like I was standing still.
They were all around me some came pretty close
and looked me in the eye, great company.

7-30-93 7:PM   50:07.61   41:56.01   W.P. #4 1244 n.m.
    Winds have died down to nothing. Amazing how
fast the seas get calm after the wind dies down.
Will need to turn on the running lights tonight

It's pretty clear to the horizon. Clouds are up high in the sky. This is the end of the seventh day out of Trepassey and thirty-third from Plymouth.

7-31-1993   8 AM   49:54.79   41:28.44   #4 1234 NM
Pretty slow going. Only made ten mi. in last twelve hours. A slight breeze, 1-5 KTS. Seas are quite calm. Took the genoa jib down and have it in the cockpit. No sails up. Just sitting here slowly rocking like in a big cradle. Having breakfast. The last of the eggs I bought in Trepassey and "Fantastic" falafel, both fried with real butter in my cast iron fry pan, and black coffee. Slept most of the night down below, port bunk.

7-31   8:30 PM   50:08.85   41:04.21   #4 1213 NM
No wind! But, basically drifted twenty-one mi. all day. The calm feels good. Fixed the genoa this morning. Triple sewed two feet of seam with Dacron thread I got from the sailmaker in St. John's. Also put some two-inch sail tape over the sewing spot on both sides. I am amazed at the tape, once you put it on and rub it good it sticks like crazy. Hope it lasts? Wished I had a roll or two when I first started out

it's pretty clear to the horizon clouds are up high in the sky. This is the end of the seventh day out of Trepassey and thirty third from Plymouth.

7-31 1993 8:AM 49:54.79 41:25.44 #4 1234 N.M.
Pretty slow going only made ten mi in last twelve hours. A slight breeze 1-5 KTS. seas are quite calm. Took the genoa jib down and have it in the cockpit, no sails up, just sitting here slowly rocking like in a big cradle. Having breakfast, the last of the eggs I bought in Trepassey and "Fantastic" falafel, both fried with real butter in my cast iron fry pan and black coffee. Slept most of the night down below, port bunk.

7-31 8:30 PM 50:08.85 41:04.21 #4 1213 N.mi.
"No wind! But basicly drifted twenty one mi all day. The calm feels good. Fixed the genoa this morning trysple sewed two feet of seam with dacron that I got from the sailmaker in St John. Also put some two inch sail tape over the sewing spot on both sides. I am amazed at the tape, once you put it on and rub it good it sticks like crazy. Hope it lasts? Wished I had a roll or two when I first started out

158

but never knew about it before. Both sails
flapping around all day waiting for a breeze.
Good visibility all day. Some sun was trying
to poke through the clouds today in streaks
off to the east. Awesomely glorious out here.
Haven't seen any ships since the one on the first
day out. Happy about that but who knows what went
by when I could only see the hand in front of my
face. A little breeze came up about an hour
ago out of the north. Finally some wind in the
sails 10-15 kts. Am on port tack, beam reach.
The birds have all took to wing after sitting around
all day watching me. I filled the pressure cooker
with potatoes and carrots this afternoon. That should
last me a couple of days. The rice ran out yesterday.
Soup with lots of rice. Now potatoes, carrots and
soup for a while. I'm all bundled up again with
lots of clothing, slicker and boots. It's a pretty cool
wind. Ran the engine for an hour at slow RPM
to charge batteries. Will need lights again tonight.
Don't turn them on when visibility is low and
stormy. Would love a bath!

8-1-93   6:30 AM   50:16.51   40:22.86   #4 1186 NM
Cockpit, sleeping. Tied wheel off. Coffee, potatoes, carrots,

but never knew about it before. Both sails flapping around all day waiting for a breeze. Good visibility all day, some sun was trying to poke through the clouds today in streaks off to the east. Awesomely glorious out here. Havent seen any ships since the one on the first day out, happy about that but who knows what went by when I could only see the hand in front of my face. A little breeze came up about an hour ago out of the north finally some wind in the sails 10-15 kts. am on port tack beam reach. The birds have all took to wing after sitting around all day watching me. I filled the pressure cooker with potatoes and carrots this afternoon that should last me a couple of days, The rice ran out yesterday. Soup with lots of rice. Now potatoes, carrots and soup for a while. Im all bundled up again with lots of clothing, slicker & boots its a pretty cool wind. Ran the engine for an hour at slow r.p.m. to charge batteries will need lights again tonight, don't turn them on when visibility is low and stormy. Would love a bath!

3-1-93 6:30AM   50:16.5' 40:22.86 #4 1186 N.Mi
Cockpit sleeping, tired wheel off, coffee potatoes carrots

160

falafel in frying pan, breakfast. Saw a ship on
northern horizon, headed west. Not a good sign.
8-2-93 7 AM   50:09.47   38:11.29   WP#4 1115 NM
Seventy-one mi. since yesterday morning. Rough
night and rough yesterday afternoon too. Roughest
yet. Came out of the north fast. Gale, 40 mi. per
hour and more big seaways. Then switched
to southwest. Took the main down right
after breakfast yesterday and shortened the
jib again for the night and backed it like
before. Like a roller coaster ride. Am towing
a small cone off the stern about a hundred
or so feet back. I think it helps keep
me more stable coming off the wave tops.
Last night, Aug. first, Margi and I were supposed
to light candles and spend some
spiritual time together. Too rough for candles!
End of 10th day
8-2 5 PM 50:27.18 37:33.00 #4 1085
Made thirty miles since breakfast. Just
baked some cinnamon rolls and bread sticks
out of pizza dough. Fairly calm. Fog is settling
in. The storm of last night, the worst so
far, left some pretty big rollers that throughout
the day have turned into low rollers.
The weather has turned warmer. I must have

falafil in frying pan, breakfast. Saw a ship on
northern horizon headed west. Not a good sign

8-2-93 7-Am   50:09.47 38:11.29 WP #4 1115 N.Mi

Seventy one mi since yesterday morning. Rough
night and rough yesterday afternoon too. Roughest
yet. Came out of the north fast. Gale, 40 mi per
hour and more big seaways then switched
to south west, took the main down right
after breakfast yesterday and shortened the
jib again for the night and backed it like
before. Like a rollercoaster ride. Am towing
a small core off the stearn about a hundred
or so feet back, I think it helps keep
me more stable comming off the wave tops.
    Last night, Aug. first, Margie and I were supposed
to light candles ~~together~~ and spend some
spiritual time togeather, to rough for candles!

END of
10th DAY
8-2-5:PM   50:27.18 37:33.00 #4 1085
    Made thirty miles since breakfast. Just
baked some cinamon rolls and bread sticks
out of pizza dough. Fairly calm, fog is settling
in. The storm of last night, the worst so
far, left some pretty big rollers that through-
-out the day have turned into low rollers.
The weather has turned warmer, I must have

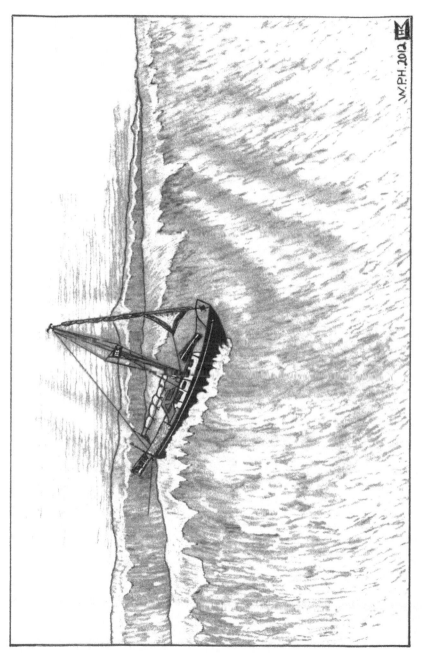

164

crossed over into the Gulf Stream. The air
and water are warmer. This is certainly the
place to be if you want to find out what's
going on in your head. The only communication
is with myself. The thought of doing one
more week out here is giving me the blues.
Thought I could make it across in twentyone
days but see now that that is not
going to happen. Four weeks out here instead
of three is a depressing thought.

Mind over mind, the balance point to find.
 Last night in the storm I lay on the cabin
sole for awhile wondering if the boat would
hold up in the pounding. Tonight looks much
better.

8-3-93 11:30 AM Didn't take a bearing.
A beautiful morning clear, the first sunrise
I actually saw the sun! A bit nippy around
the edges though. Wind out of the north-north-
east. A wall of dark clouds is moving towards me
from the north, the sun a memory through
the low gray cover.
 I did see quite a few jet contrails running
along my course, some of them to my north

crossed over into the Gulfstream the air and water are warmer. This is certainly the place to be if you want to find out whats goin' on in your head. The only comunacation is with myself. The thought of doing one more week out here is giving me the blues. I thought I could make it accross in twenty one days but see now that that is not going to happen. Four weeks out here instead of three is a depressing thought.

Mind over mind, The balance point to find. Last night in the storm I lay on the cabin ~~sole~~ for a while wondering if the boat would hold up in the pounding. Tonight looks much better

8-3-93 11:30 AM didn't take a bearing
A beautiful morning, clear, the first sunrise I actualy saw the sun! A bit nippy around the edges though. Wind out of the north-north--east a wall of dark clouds is moving twords me from the north the sun a memory through the low greay cover.

I did see quite a few jet contrails running along my course, some of them to my north

166

some to my south. The ones to the north
are headed to Europe - east, and the ones to
the south are headed to Canada or the States,
west. Can't see the planes. Only a bit of silver
reflection now and then.

Last night around eleven is when this
north wind began, and the fog lifted and
dissipated. A full moon lit up the sea like
magic. The stars, the first I've seen, shone
crisp and clear and bright, like I could reach out
and touch them. Like I had just painted them
and at arms reach could add another or move
them around.

I also saw the third ship to the north
also headed west like the others, about four
to five miles off. Tried to reach them on
channel sixteen VHF, but no response. I'm
sure they don't even know I'm here.
The rest of the night was a beat off course
about fifteen degrees to the south. Light wind
5-10. Made some progress until about four
AM. The wind died. Went down below
for a snooze. Back up at six with the same
beat. Just visited by a group of dolphins.
Have seen quite a few almost every day.

some to my south. The ones to the north
are headed to Europe - east, and the ones to
the south are headed to Canada or the States,
west. Can't see the planes only a bit of silou
reflection now and then.

Last night around eleven is when this
north wind began and the fog lifted and
disapated. A full moon lit up the sea like
magic. The stars, the first I've seen, shone
crisp and clear and bright, like I could reach out
and touch them, like I had just painted them
and at arms reach could add another or move
them around.

I also saw the third ship to the north
also headed west like the others, about four
to five miles off. I tried to reach them on
channel sixteen VHF but no response, I'm
shure they don't even know I'm here.

The rest of the night was a beat off course
about fifteen degrees to the south. Light wind
5-10 made some progress until about four
a.m. the wind died went down below
for a snooze, back up at six with the same
beat. Just visited by a group of dolphins,
have seen quite a few almost every day

168

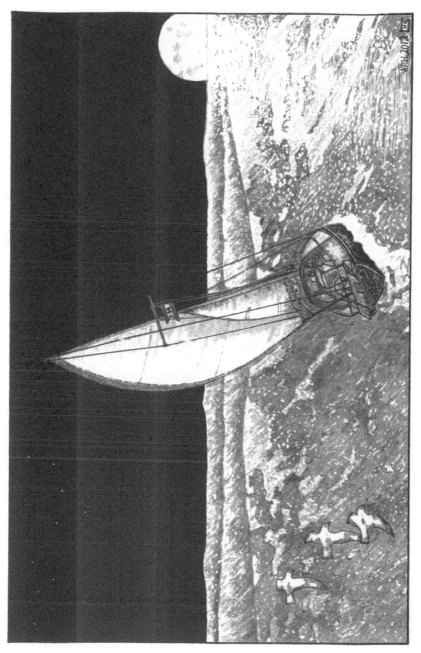

They show up and play in the bow wake for
a while. But, now there are hundreds of them
all around. Some are jumping all the way out
of the water. It's like being in a sea of dolphins.
They must be feeding as there are lots of
birds flying around as if waiting for scraps.
Never seen so many dolphins.
The wind just stopped and so did I. Then
just as fast started up again but shifted about
20° more northerly. I have the wheel set on
new course 84° making three or four knots.
End of 11th day
8-3-93 5 PM   50:20.08 35:55.07 WP#4 1033 NM
What a beautiful summers afternoon it turned
out to be. The only clouds in the sky are way
high up and caused by all the airline contrails.
All day back and forth they flew right over
my head. Otherwise, the sky and the sea
a beautiful blue.

Heaved to and tender does she lay,
Against the wind and blue,
As I repose for a rest,
From watch of salty spray.
And gently hear the voice of her,
The one my heart cares for,
Across the miles I hear her,
She touches me,
I smile and think no more.

they show up and play in the bow wake for
a while. But now there are hundreds of them
all around, some are jumping all the way out
of the water, it's like being in a sea of dolphins
they must be feeding as there are lots of
birds flying around as if waiting for scraps.
Never seen so many dolphins.

The wind just stopped and so did I, then
just as fast started up again but shifted about
20° more northerly I have the wheel set on
new course 84° making three or four knots.

END OF 11th DAY

8-3-93   5: PM   50:20.08 35.55.07   W.P.q 1033 N.MI.

"What a beautiful summers afternoon it turned
out to be the only clouds in the sky are way
high up and caused by all the airline contrails.
All day back and forth they flew right over
my head. Otherwise the sky and the sea
a beautiful blue.

Heaved to, and tender does she lay,
Against the wind and blue,
As I repose for a rest, from watch of salty spray.
And gently hear the voice of her, the one my
heart cares for,
Across the miles I hear her, she touches me,
I smile and think no more.

When the sun sizzles on the pond,
To rest when day is through,
My heart remembers you.

With each swell of warm desire,
Returns the glow of beeswax fire,
My heart remembers you.

My heart remembers story times,
The silliness of nursery rhymes,
The taste and glow of your lips' wine,
My heart remembers you.

I soaked up as much sun as was possible today
shedding all of my clothes, even boots and wool
socks, which have not seen the light of day
since Trepassey. My feet rejoice in the
freedom. The cockpit (wonder where that expression
came from?) was strewn with stuff drying
out. It was a cockpit today.
12th day
8-4 5 PM   50:50.80 34:34.13   972 NM to #4
Made sixty miles since early this morning.
Last night no wind. Finished dinner and took some
pictures of sunset then turned in and drifted

When the sun sizzles on the sand,
To rest when day is through,
My heart remembers you.

With each swell of warm desire,
Returns the glow of beeswax fire,
My heart remembers you.

My heart remembers story times,
The sillyness of nursery rhymes,
The taste and glow of your lips wine,
My heart remembers you.

I soaked up as much sun as was possible today
sheading all of my cloths evan boots and wool
socks which have not seen the light of day
since Trepassey and my feet rejoyceing in the
freedom. The cockpit (wonder where that expression
came from?) was strewen with stuff drying
out. It was a cockpit today.

12th day
5-4 5 PM   50'50 80   34.'34.13   972 nemi TO #4
Made sixty miles since early this morning.
Last night no wind, finished dinner and took some
pictures of sunset then turned in and drifted

with jib pulled in tight amidships and main
down. Woke up at 3:30 AM to a few wavelets
lapping on the side. The wind was just starting
to come up so I got up and put out both
sails wing and wing for a downwind run.
watched a gorgeous sunrise and full moon
fade. Hove-to around eight for breakfast
then pushed on. Stopped again for lunch.
It's difficult to stop for a break 'cause I
feel like moving on and making more headway while there's a wind. There's no way
to leave the wheel and tie it off going
down wind - monotonous - to say the
least. I've stopped now because I can't do
it anymore. I've been counting down the hours
for the last four to take a fix and eat and
rest some. Soup with garlic toast. Now with
pen, tea, and a few molasses cookies time
to reflect. The seas are 3-5, wind 15 kts.
or so. The boat rides easy hove-to. Could
spend some time and take a nap but wonder
when this easy wind and sea will change for the
worse, so I'll push on and try for a few more
miles. Rare to have conditions last for long.
Visibility about one mile in fog.

with jib pulled in tight amidships and main down. Woke up at 3:30 am to a few wave-lets lapping on the side, the wind was just starting to come up so I got up and put out both sails wing and wing for a down wind run. Watched a gorgeous sunrise and full moon fade. Hove-to around eight for breakfast then pushed on, stopped again for lunch. It's difficult to stop for a break cause I feel like moving on and making more head--way while there's a wind. There's no way to leave the wheel and tie it off going down wind — monotonous — to say the least. I've stopped now because I can't do it anymore, I've been counting down the hours for the last four to take a fix and eat and rest some. Soup with garlic toast. Now with pen, tea and a few molasses cookies time to reflect. The seas are 3-5, wind 15 KTS. or so. The boat rides easy hove-to could spend some time and take a nap but wonder when this easy wind and sea will change for the worse so I'll push on and try for a few more miles. Rare to have conditions last for long. Visability about one mile in fog.

Not looking forward to getting back at the wheel.

8-5-93   1:30 PM   51:33.59 32:45.00   WP#4 892 NM
Eight hundred ninety-two mi. to the Bloody
Foreland. Wind out of the west southwest
blowing pretty good about twenty kts. Seas
are over ten feet about forty feet apart.
I hove to about midnight and crashed in my
bunk. I didn't care if a ship did run me
down. The wind slowly picked up a little
since yesterday and holding steady. Trying
to keep a course is a murderous task.
All down wind and constantly turning the
wheel back and forth, back and forth. Her
stern goes up and tries to fall to port.
Then turn wheel to compensate. Then stern
goes up and tries to fall off to starboard,
so turn wheel to starboard to compensate.
Back and forth, back and forth. My shoulder
and neck muscles are on fire. Slept last
night 'till sunrise. It's like waking up
to a bad dream.

8-5   5 PM   Thirty-nine days out of Plymouth.
Thirteen out of Trepassey. Winds are calming down,

Not looking forward to getting back at the wheel

8-5-93 ~~1AM~~ 1:30 PM 51:33.59 32:45.10 WPT4 892 NM.
Eight hundred ninety two mi. to the Bloody
Fioreland. Wind out of the west south west
blowing pretty good about twenty kts. seas
are over ten feet about forty feet apart.
I hove to about midnight and crashed in my
bunk. I didn't care if a ship did run me
down. The wind slowly picked up a little
since yesterday and holding steady. Trying
to keep a course is a murderious task.
All down wind and constantly turning the
wheel back and forth, back and forth, her
steam goes up and tryes to fall to port
then turn wheel to compensate, then steam
goes up and trys to fall off to starboard
so turn wheel to starboard to compensate,
back and forth, back and forth. My shoulder
and neck mucles are on fire. Slept last
night till sunrise. Its like wakening up
to a bad dream.

8.5 5 PM Thirty nine days out of Plymouth,
~~Fifteen~~ out of Trepassey. Winds are calming down
Thirteen

178

harder and harder to stay at the wheel.
Dolphins all around me again and riding
what's left of the seaway. The dolphins
and the birds my only company, and the songs
in my head play over and over relentlessly.
I forcefully sing out to break what ever
rhythm that's playing over and over and over
with some new rhythm. Have been reading
"Zen and the Art of Motorcycle Maintenance" and
find myself also trying to find quality in the
vastness of quantity. When the dolphins are
here and the birds are circling about, it's as if
we are traveling along together, and their presence
has a calming effect on me. I feel the quality
of the moments. The picture seems complete,
life, moving forward, each of us doing our own
thing, harmoniously, and the calming rhythm of
the sea.

8-6   6:30 PM   51:25.81   30:42.74   WP#4 826 NM
Light winds for the last twenty-four hours.
Last night about 2:30AM went down below and
crashed. Didn't care what happened to me. Hove
to and went below. Woke about seven a.m.
to the nightmare of still being here!!

179

harder and harder to stay ~~~~ at the wheel. Dolphins all around me again and riding whats left of the sea-way. The dolphins and the birds my only company and the songs in my head play over and over relentlessly. I forcefully sing out to break whatever rythem thats playing over and over and over with some new rythem. Have been reading "Zen and the art of motorcycle maintenance" and find myself also trying to find quality in the vastness of quanity. When the dolphins are here and the birds are circling about, it's as if we are traveling along togeather and their presence has a calming effect on me, I feel the quality of the moments, the picture seems complete, life, moving forward, each of us doing our own thing, harmoniously and the calming rythem of the sea.

8-6   6:30PM   51:25.81   30:42.74 W.A.#4 806 NM

Lite winds for the last twenty four hours. Last night about 2:30AM went down below and crashed; didnt care what happened to me, have to and went below. Woke about seven a.m. to the night mare of still being here!!

The only way out is back on the wheel,
Pitching and yawing, all that I feel.
Sitting then standing, sitting than stand,
Crying out for my Mother --- dry land.

My neck and my shoulders fiery-sore,
I say to myself, I can't take it no more.

Watching the compass swing this way then that.
Ties chaffing my stubble from the so'wester hat.
Chaffing my brow, chaffing my sleeve,
Chaffing my nerves, my sanity flees.
Scream at it, fight it, you'll not get me down.
And then, look! The dolphins, all around.
Urging me forward, playfully bound,
Just when I needed, they found.

*1AM

From the deck the horizon is blurred,
Where the sky meets the sea who knows,
I find myself in a sphere of my own,
Like one of those glass balls with snow.
The dampness all around,
Its mission, cleaning and preening
The air of impurities,

181

The only way out is back on the wheel,
Pitching and yawing, all that I feel.
Sitting then standing, sitting then stand,
Crying out for my Mother;... dry land.

My neck and my shoulders firey-sore,
I say to myself I can't take it no more.

Watching the compass swing this way then that.
Ties chaffing my stubble from the so-wester
hat.
Chaffing my brow, chaffing my sleeve, chaffing
my nerves; my sanity, flees.
Scream at it, fight it, you'll not get
me down,
And then, look! the dolphins, all around,
Urging me forward, playfully bound,
Just when I needed, they found.

1AM
From the deck the horizon is blurred,
where the sky meets the sea who knows,
I find myself in a sphere of my own like
one of those glass balls with snow.
The dampness all around, its mission,
cleaning and preaning the air of impurities

182

Condensing on the rigging and in the cabin,
Running, dripping,
Gravity trying to return it back to its source.
The birds sit all around me as we wait for a shift in wind,
And the cycle to begin once more,
First as gentle ripples,
Then growing to a tempest roar.

❀

8 AM   8-7
Foggy for the third day or fourth. I've lost count.
Light wind all night 5-10. Turned in
about 2:30 AM, hove to, main down, dripping wet.
Tightened genoa to amidships.
Woke about 5:30. Feel like I'm in a dungeon,
doing time. The fog not as close in as last
evening. I can see a few miles or so. The
birds or most of them are circling around.
I feel a change in the air, not so wet and heavy.
In no hurry to do anything but eat, read some,
drink coffee. Close to the halfway point.

No rest for the weary, and weary is I,
Of sails pointing up through anodized sky.
Of watching on wheel through fogginess peel,
With want of some slumber to feel.

condensing on the rigging and in the cabin,
running, dripping, gravity trying to return
it back to its source. The birds sit all
around me as we wait for a shift in the
wind and the cycle to begin once more,
first as gentle ripples, then growing to
a tempest roar.

8:AM 8-7
Foggy for the third day or forth I've lost
count. Light wind all night 5-10. Turned in
about 2:30 AM, hove-to, main down, dripping wet,
tightened, genoa to amid ships.
Woke about 5:30, feel like I'm in a dungeon
doing time. The fog not as close in as last
evening, I can see a few miles or so, the
birds or most of them are circling around.
I feel a change in the air, not so wet and heavy.
I'm in no hurry to do anything but eat, read some,
drink coffee. Close to the half way point
No rest for the weary, and weary is d,
Of sails pointing up through anodized sky.
Of watching on wheel through fogginess peel,
With want of some slumber to feel.

184

With chat and reply, by the same guy.
Of unfinished song that keeps whirring along,
A mind of its own, so I leave it alone,
And think of loved ones at home.

With thoughts here of you, my invisible crew,
the day slips away on its own.

It's the visions of thee that set my mind free,
From this dungeon, and its moan,
And allows me to feel safe,
When so far from home.

If home is where the heart is,
Then homelessness I shall never fear,
For if home is where the heart is,
Then I'm home when I think of you here.

I empathize with prisoners and what
might keep them going, possibilities. Perhaps
it's nothing more than possibilities that keeps
us all going.

8-7 noon   5:43.82 29:33.54 WP#4 779 NM C 83°
The sun is out hooray!!! Fog cleared out
around nine. Wind came up out of sou'west.

With chat and reply, by the same guy.
Of unfinished song that keeps whirring along,
A mind of its own, so I leave it alone and
think of loved ones at home.

With thoughts here of you, my invisible
crew, the day slipps away on its own.

Its the visions of ~~thee~~ that set my mind free,
from this dungeon, and its moan,
And allows me to feel safe, when so far
from home.

If home is where the heart is, then homelessness
I shall never fear, for if home is where the
heart is, then Im home when I think you here.

I empithize with ~~prisoners~~ prisoners and what
might keep them going, possibilitys, perhaps
its nothing more than possibilitys that keeps
us all going.

8-7 noon   51:43.82   29.33.54   W.P.D 779 N.M.   C-85°
The sun is out hooray!!! Fog cleared out
around nine, wind came up out of so-west

186

CHAPTER 14

10-15 kts. Back on the wheel, down wind, wing
and wing. Passed the halfway point.
End of 15th day
8-7   5:30 PM   51:49.18   29:02.03 WP #4 759 NM C 83°
The sun was out for about three hours. Wind
increased steadily all afternoon, about 20 now.
Blowing pretty good, too rough to wing and wing.
Took down main. Rolled genoa in about half,
backed to amidship and tight. Set wheel (tied off)
with starboard weather helm, (turned to the right
slightly) on a more easterly-south-easterly
course. I'm in the cockpit port side in bean
bag chair, cozy. This is more like it but I'm
heading for Spain. I'll ride this for awhile then
switch the whole rig around and head north
for a while later on if the wind holds.
Good to get a break from the wheel!!!

Sunday morning   8-8-93   9 AM
This strikes me as serious business being out
here. One false move and I could be in the soup,
as they say. It's pretty rough and blowing 25-30 kts.
as a guess. As a usual rule, to relieve myself,
#1 that is, I go out on the rail and lean my
left shoulder against the main mast standing rigging

10-15 back on the wheel, down wind, wing
and wing, passed the half way point.

End of 15th day

8-7   5:30PM.   51:49.18 29:02.03 $^{wp.}$#4 759 NM $^{c-83°}$
The sun was out for about three hours, wind
increased steadily all afternoon, about 20 now
blowing pretty good to rough to wing and wing.
Took down main and rolled genoa in about half
backed to amid ships and tight, set wheel (tied off)
with starboard weather helm, (turned to the right
slightly) on a more easterly-south-easterly
course. I'm in the cockpit port side in bean
bag chair, cozey. This is more like it but I'm
heading for Spain. I'll ride this for a-while then
switch the whole rig around and head north
for a-while latter on if the wind holds.
Good to get a break from the wheel!!!

Sunday morning, 8-8-93 9:AM
This strikes me as serious buisness being out
here, one false move and I could be in the soup
as they say. It's pretty rough and blowing 25-30 KTS
as a guess. As a usual rule to relieve myself,
1 that is, I go out on the rail and lean my
left shoulder against the main mast standing rigging

190

on the leeward side (that is the side sheltered
from the wind) and wrap my left arm around
it and proceed with things, having two hands
free for the job at hand, buttons, zippers and alike.
This morning, being a little rushed, the boat
caught a bigger than usual wave and almost
threw me over right in the middle of things.
Luckily, all of the right muscles worked in unison
and I did get to finish without having to go
below and change my pants.
I have a ¾ inch nylon safety line that I wear
around my waist, most of the time, while in the
cockpit and when I go forward to rig the spinnaker
pole for wing and wing and to tend to anything
else that needs attention. But, I was in a hurry
and full of confidence this AM and forgot to
put it on. Won't happen again!
It's a thrilling thing to be out on the bow
in a blow and look back at the boat pressing
onward in thirty foot seas, like riding a
surf board, hanging ten but, actually hanging two,
cheeks that is, blue water, green peaks,
white streaks.

on the leeward side (that is the side sheltered from the wind) and wrap my left arm around it and procede with things, having two hands free for the job at hand, buttons, zippers and a-like. This morning, being a little rushed, the boat caught a bigger than usual wave and almost threw me over right in the middle of things. Luckily all of the right mussels worked in unison and I did get to finish without having to go below and change my pants. I have a 3/4 inch nylon safty line that I wear around my wrist most of the time while in the cockpit and when I go forward to the spinnaker pole for wing and wing and to tend to any thing else that needs attention but was in a hurry and full of confidence this a.m. and forgot to put it on. Won't happen again!

Its a thrilling thing to be out on the bow in a blow and look back at the boat pressing onward in thirty foot seas, like riding a surfboard, hanging ten, but actually hanging two, cheeks that is; blue water, green peaks, white streaks.

8-8-93   11 AM   51:55.88 28:03.43 WP#4 723 NM C102°
Just put new batteries in GPS. No alkaline
left. Put in Eveready Classics. Hope they last
awhile. Just turned the chart over and now
I am able to see the British Isles and the
European coast from Norway to Spain.
South-west still blowing thirty plus. Seas are
also thirty plus. I'm surrounded by white
topped blue gray waves. Wind blown and
beautiful, and I at the mercy of them. It's ok
though. We just ride like the birds up and
over each on coming wall of wet.
Concern for my dinghy though. It's hanging
over the stern on 1" galvanized pipe
davits which I made, and every now and then
takes a hit from the transom going down
suddenly, until the dinghy slams onto the water.
One of the stainless steel clamps that hold
the pipes to the aft. cleats had snapped under
the pressure, and I had to ransack around
looking for a spare, which I found and put
on, fearing if another one went the dinghy would
flail around and do some damage. I watch
them nervously. Am down below now in
port-settee bunk reading and writing and
listening the the wind. Seems to be building

8-8-93 11:AM   51:55.88 28:03.43   WP. #4   C-102°
                                                 723 N.M

Just put new batteries in G.P.S. No alkaline
left put in everready classics hope they last
a-while. Just turned the chart over and now
I am able to see the British Isles and the
European coast from Norway to Spain.
South-west still blowing thirty plus, seas are
also thirty plus. I'm surrounded by white
topped blue grey waves. Wind-blown and
beautiful and I at the mercy of them. It's ok
though we just ride like the birds up and
over each on comming wall of wet.
Concerned for my dinghy though it's hanging
over the stearn on 1" galvinized pipe
davits which I made, and every now and then
takes a hit from the transom going down
suddenly until the dinghy slams onto the water.
one of the stainless steel clamps that hold
the pipes to the aft cleats has snapped under
the pressure and I had to ran sack around
looking for a spare which I found and put
on fearing if another one went the dinghy would
flail around and do some damage. I watch
them nervously. Am down below now in
port-settee bunk reading and writing and
listening to the wind, seems to be building

strength. Every now and then I slide back
the hatch and poke my head out and look
around. Nothing to see though, but blue
walls of white-streaked water when at the
bottom of the troughs, and at the top of
the peaks, row after row of them. The air
is heavy with wind blown wet, and luckily
no ships. Although ships are not the only
concern. There is also the thought of hitting
some big floating object like a tree or floating
timber, which might poke a hole in the thin
fiberglass skin.
End of 16th Day
8-8-93 5:30 PM   51:43.92 26:11.00 WP#4 717 C80°
Took a nap after lunch, about a four and
a half hour nap, and woke to calmer conditions.
The wind is down to about twenty and the
seas less whipped up, less water blowing
about. Cooked up some brown and wild rice,
mixed in a can of red kidney beans, olive oil,
a little butter, Braggs (soy sauce), pepper and green
beans - made it complete. Now having tea with
some powdered milk and four Oreo cookies. Hope the
Oreos hold out. Rested all day. Made little
headway since 11 AM.

strength. Every now and then I slide back the hatch and poke my head out and look around. Nothing to see though but blue walls of white streaked water, when at the bottom of the troughs and at the tops of the peaks row after row of them. The air is heavy with wind blown wet, and luckely no ships. Although ships are not the only concern, there is also the thought of hitting some big floating object like a tree or floating timber which might poke a hole in the thin fiberglass skin.

8-8-93 5:30 PM   51:43.92   26:11.00   WATER 717 C 80°

Took a nap after lunch, about a four and a half hour nap, and woke to calmer conditions. The wind is down to about twenty and the seas less whipped up, less water blowing about. Cooked up some brown and wild rice, mixed in a can of red kidney beans, olive oil, a little butter, Braggs (soy sauce), pepper and green beans made it complete. Now having tea with some powdered milk and four oreo cookies. Hope the Oreo's hold out. Rested all day made little headway. since 11 AM.

8-9-1993 8 AM
About midnight last night reset genoa to
port and unrolled to about eight or so feet.
Wind about 20-25 and started to make headway
again. After dinner last night dozed off
again and drifted. Stayed awake in cockpit
all night keeping watch from midnight 'till now.
Sky steely grey. Fog high off the water.
Visibility about five miles. Large seaways.
17th day over
8-9 5:30 PM   51:43.92 26:11.00 #4 665 C 80°
Spent the last seventeen hours or so traveling
off course to the southeast to avoid going
down wind. Although the boat is heading southeast,
the wind is pushing me sideways northeast
also. It's like slip sliding away, as Paul
Simon would say and now I'll probably have
that song stuck in my head all night. Still
large seaways. Wind twenty to twenty-five
and thirty in gusts. Steering just off down
wind to starboard. Genoa about half out and
seas rushing under starboard rear quarter,
doing four to five kts.

8-9-1993 8:AM

About midnite last night re-set genoa to port and unrolled to about eight or so feet. Wind about 20-25 and started to make headway again. After dinner last night dosed off again and drifted. Stayed awake in cockpit all night keeping watch from midnite till now. Sky steely grey, fog high off the water visibility about five miles, large sea ways.

17 THOU OVER

8-9   5:30 PM   51° 43.9 d   26° 11.00 #4 665 ⁵80°

Spent the last seventeen hours or so traveling off course to the south-east to avoid going down wind. Although the boat is heading south-east the wind is pushing me side ways north-east also. It's like slip sliding away, as Paul Simon would say and now I'll probably have that song stuck in my head all night. Still large sea ways, wind twenty to twenty five and thirty in gusts. Steering just off down wind to starboard, genoa about half out and seas rushing under starboard rear quarter, doing four to five kts..

8-10 9AM   52:10.24   25:48.73 WP #4 641 NM C80°
Gave up the wheel about 9:00 last night and
went below after rolling up the genoa to a small
triangle and setting tight amidships and tying off
the wheel to a little starboard helm. Tired and
wet, took off all the foul weather gear and boots
and hit the bunk. Woke up about four a.m.
and laid there, sleep gone, looking at the Chelsea
clock softly illuminated by the small gimbaled oil
lamp which I keep going all night as to have some
light to see by if needed. Laid there for an hour
contemplating the daily grind and trying to avoid
what I know must be done, get back on the wheel.
My stomach turning and tightening with anxiety.
Finally after the sun was up for about an hour,
got up, put on the gear, grabbed some dried prunes
and a few crackers to get the system charged a bit,
and felt better in the fresh air. Drifted about
twenty-four miles closer in the last twelve hours,
but sailed the last three of those at the wheel.
Starboard running reach like yesterday seeing the
wind still holding out of the south-west at twenty
to twenty-five kts. Large seaway still, twenty
to twenty-five feet.

8-10 9:AM 52:10.24 25:48.73 WP#4 641 NM. 80°

Gave up the wheel about 9:00 last night and
went below after rolling up the genoa to a small
triangle and setting tight amidships and tying off
the wheel to a little starboard helm. Tired and
wet, took off all the foul weather gear and boots
and hit the bunk. Woke up about four a.m.
and lyed there, sleep gone, looking at the Chelsea
clock softly illuminated by the small gimbled oil
lamp which I keep going all night as to have some
light to see by if needed. Layed there for an hour
contemplating the daily grind and trying to avoid
what I know must be done, get back on the wheel.
My stomach turning and tightening with anxiety.
Finally after the sun was up for about an hour
got up put on the gear grabbed some dried prunes
and a few crackers to get the system charged a bit
and felt better in the fresh air. Drifted about
twenty four miles closer in the last twelve hours
but sailed the last three of those at the wheel,
starboard running reach like yesterday seeing the
wind still holding out of the southwest at twenty
to twenty five kts. Large seaways still, twenty
to twenty five feet.

200

Like a cork well agitated up and down the opposites,
One must learn to smooth the way,
Let the rhythm carry you peaceful
In the turbid day.

8-10   3 PM
The sky is heavy and gray over me and
lighter, puffy white clouds on the horizon to
the north. On a port reach. A few hours
ago, the wind shifted from southwest to west
to north in a matter of minutes. I was running
with the genoa nearly out on a starboard
running reach and all of a sudden the wind
hit the back of the sail. I had to scramble
to switch the genoa and reef it in some, and
then reef it in some more as the north wind
increased. It has been five or six days since
a wind shift. And the routine of it and being
at the wheel with it was wearing on me. Finding
it more and more difficult with each passing
hour. Now, with the wheel tied off with some
port weather helm and zipping along at five
knots plus, like being set free!
Some sun peeked through for about thirty
minutes, then dark clouds from the north
roaring south dumped some rain for thirty
minutes or so.
The seas are totally confused now, where
an hour ago they were just confused.
Heaping and jumping and crashing into each

like a cork well agitated up and down the
opposite, one must learn to smooth the way, let
the rythem carry you peaceful in the turbed day

810 3 PM
The sky is heavy and gray over me and
lighter, puffy-white clouds on the horizon to
the north. On a port reach. A few hours
ago the wind shifted from south-west to west
to north in a matter of minutes. I was running
with the genoa nearly out on a starboard
running reach and all of a sudden the wind
hit the back of the sail and I had to scramble
to switch the genoa and reef it in some and
then reef it in some more as the north wind
increased. It has been five or six days since
a wind shift. And the routine of it and being
at the wheel with it was wearing on me, finding it more and more difficult with each passing
hour. Now with the wheel tied off with some
port weather helm and zipping along at five
knots plus, like being set free!
Some sun poked through for about thirty
minutes then dark clouds from the north
roaring south, dumped some rain for thirty
minutes or so.
The seas are totally confused now, where
an hour ago they were just confused.
Heaping and jumping and crashing into each

202

other, from the southwest, from the west
and from the north. Now, with the north
wind intensifying, it's a cauldron.
The Kandahar is proving herself a well found boat.
Handling herself with ease, she just digs her nose
in and says, "Move over! Coming through!" and giving
me quite a ride in the process.
The north wind is chilly compared with the
southwest of the previous days, and a refreshing
change. It blew off the fog, and for the first
time in a week, at least, I am able to see the
blue horizon.
This morning I noticed another species of bird
has joined the procession, smaller than the
seabirds that have been with me since Trepassey.
About the size of a large swallow, dark with a
white spot on its back. Haven't seen any of
these before. I'm about six hundred mi. off the
coast of Ireland. Will be 2/3rds of the way across
tomorrow. Had a good scare earlier. One
of those large, confused waves broke right
at the stern, partially filling and almost tearing
off the eight-foot pram dingy, bending the
pipe davit pretty good. Hope the north wind
keeps up for a while. Like being on vacation
being off the wheel. Making good time.

other, from the south west, from the west and from the north, now with the north wind intensifying, it's a cauldron.

The Kandahar is proving herself a well found boat, handeling herself with ease, she just digs her nose in and says move over, comming through and giving me quite a ride in the process.

The north wind is chilly compared with the south-west of the previous days and a refreshing change. It blew off the fog and for the first time in a week, at least, I am able to see the blue horizon.

This morning I noticed another species of bird has joined the procession, smaller than the sea birds that have been with me since Frapassey about the size of a large swallow, dark with a white spot on its back, havent seen any of these before. I'm about six hundred mi. of the coast of Ireland, will be 2/3² of the way across tomorrow. Had a good scare earlyer, one of those large, confused, sea ways broke right at the steam partally filling and almost tearing off the eight foot pram dingy, bending the pipe davit pretty good. Hope the north wind keeps up for a-while, like being on vacation being off the wheel. Making good time

8-10-1993 5:30 PM 52:23.69 24:53.88 WP#4 605 NM C82°
 The batteries gave out for the G.P.S. - now using
LORAN. I checked my position with the LORAN
against the G.P.S. and they both read about the
same. The LORAN stands for Long Range Navigation
and was developed (as far as I know), during the
last world war. It consists of a string of
radio towers positioned along the coasts
sending out radio waves on a certain frequency.
The receiver on my boat and on other boats,
ships, and planes too, I believe, picks up
this signal from as many towers as within
its range, cross references the distance and angle,
calculates its position from the
received information, and displays its position in
longitude and latitude. The newer G.P.S. uses
radio signals from satellites in fixed positions
above the earth. The LORAN receiver is mounted down
below and uses power from the boat's two
twelve volt batteries and picks up signals
from a whip antenna, like
an old car antenna, about four feet long,
mounted on the stern railing, which is
outside of the cone of the metal standing-rigging,
which holds up the masts and can cause
interference with the radio signals.

205

8-10-1993 - 5:30PM   52:23.69   24:53.88 WP#4 605 NM C82°

The bateries gave out for the G.P.S., now using
LORAN. I checked the my position with the loran
against the G.P.S. and they both read about the
same. The loran stands for Long range navigation
and was developed (as far as I know,) during the
last world war. It consists of a string of
radio towers positioned along the coasts
sending out radio waves on a certain frequency
and the reciever on my boat and on other boats,
ships and planes too, I believe, pick up
this signal from as many towers as within
its range and cross references the distance and angle
and calculates its position from the
recieved information and displays its position in
longitude and latitude. Where the GPS uses
radio signals from satilites in fixed positions
above the earth. The loran reciever is mounted down
below and uses power from the boats two
twelve volt batteries and picks up signals
from a whip antena, like
an old car antena, about four feet long
mounted on the stearn railing which is
outside of the cone of the metal standing rigging,
which holds up the mast and which can cause
interferance with radio signals. ⑨

206

I've had the LORAN for about five years.
which cost me then about three hundred dollars,
and it is about twice the size of a pack of cigarettes.
The G.P.S. on the other hand, which I just bought
just to have a back up system, cost almost
eight hundred and is portable, using nine double-
A batteries (alkaline). The G.P.S. is about six
inches by nine inches by two inches thick
and needs to be held out side the standing
rigging cone in order to be sure of a correct
reading. This is not as easy as it sounds
in rough blowing conditions. I keep it
in a large plastic bag to protect it from
getting wet and must be at the stern rail
and hold it above my head in order to
get a signal. It takes several minutes
for it to pick up two or more satellites.
Back home while cruising around, the LORAN
has been a real life saver especially in Maine
in the fog, amongst the rocky coast. With
a chart of the area I could plot my position
within thirty feet, find a buoy or a harbor
entrance without any visibility. The greatest
danger being running into another boat or
getting your prop entangled in a lobster

I've had the loran for about five years wich cost me then about three hundred dollars, and it is about twice the size of a pack of cigarettes. The G.P.S. on the other hand, witch I just bought, just to have a back up system, cost almost eight hundred and is portable, using nine double A batteries (alkaline). The G.P.S. is about six inches by nine inches by two inches thick and needs to be held out side the standing rigging core in order to be sure of a correct reading. This is not as easy as its sounds in rough blowing conditions. I keep it in a large plastic bag to protect it from getting wet and must be at the steam rail and hold it above my head in order to get a signal and it takes several minutes for it to pick up two or more satitities. Back home while crusing around, the loran has been a real life saver especially in Maine in the fog, amongst the rocky coast. With a chart of the area I could plot my position with in thirty feet. I find a bouy or a harbor entrance without any visability the greatest danger being running into another boat or getting your prop entangled in a lobster

pot line (or warp), as they call them.
Well, hope this LORAN will work the rest of the
way. Good wind all afternoon.
Wednesday   (LORAN)
8-11 5:30 PM   53:09.07   23:23.29 537 NM
Large seaways. Really rough. Roughest yet.
Wind came around out of the north-west and increased
all day. Genoa rolled up to small trysail and
pulled in tight amidships. Wheel tied with
port weather helm. Spent all day below on cabin
sole on bean bag chair; only place comfortable.
Tough to concentrate on reading, need both hands to
hang on when on my feet. Seas forty feet plus
wind about fifty.
I see that I am being blown pretty far north
on this port tack so will go and change wheel
over to starboard. Wind seems to be slowly coming
around to the west.
7 PM
 Just got down below again. Spent an hour
topside. Changed the wheel over to starboard weather
helm. Seas are huge and angry looking. Lots
of foam blowing off peaks. I'm towing a
small cone about a hundred feet, maybe a
hundred fifty feet off of starboard stern cleat.

pot line (or warps) as they call them.
Well, hope this loran will work the rest of the
way. Good wind all afternoon.

Wednesday
8-11   5;30 PM   53;09.07   (LORAN) 23;23.29   WP #4   53 > N.M. C 85°

Large seaways, really rough, roughest yet,
wind came around out of the north-west and increasing
all day. Genoa rolled up to small try sail and
pulled in tight amid-ships, wheel tied with
port weather helm. spent all day below on cabin
sole on bean bag chair, only place comfortable,
tough to concentrate on reading, need both hands to
hang on when on my feet. Seas forty feet plus
wind about fifty.

I see that I am being blown pretty far north
on this port tack so will go and change wheel
over to starboard, wind seems to be slowly coming
around to the west

7;PM

Just got down below again spent an hour
topside, changed the wheel over to starboard weather
helm, seas are huge and angry looking, lots
of foam flowing off of peaks, I'm towing a
small cone about a hundred feet maybe a
hundred fifty feet off of starboard stern cleat.

WPK2012

8-12 4:30 AM
What a night. Unbelievable. Spent all night
on the cabin sole with cushions on both sides
of me and hanging on. The wind was screamin'
all night. The boat would rise up and
fall out from under me like being pushed
off of every crest and coming down with
a thud throwing me against the bulkhead
and back down again. Every one I thought
was going to be the one to roll us over.
So thankful for daylight. The seas are
absolutely huge. Must be sixty feet
or more and the winds a full gale at
least sixty also. Scary!! Poked my
head out of the hatch and held on tight,
and watched the whole scene for a while.
As the waves came up in a peak the wind
would blow the top over and it would
break, and when we would come up
with the peak, the wind would try to
blow us over and the stern would come
almost straight up and the wave would
break under the tail pushing the nose down
and we, me and the boat, would try surfing but couldn't
surf as fast as the water is racing, and thank
God for the cone and its rode, to hold us

8-12 4:30 AM

Wat a night, unbeleavable, spent all night
on the cabin sole with cushins on both sides
of me and hangin on, the wind was screamin'
all night and the boat would rise up and
fall out from under me like being pushed
off of every crest and comming down with
a thud and throw me against the bulkhead
and back down again. Everyone I thought
was going to be the one to roll us over.
So thankfull for day light, the seas are
absolutly huge, must be sixty feet
or more, and the winds a full gale at
least sixty also, scarry!! Poked my
head out of the hatch and held on tight
and watched the whole scene for a while.
As the waves come up in a peak the wind
would blow the tops over and it would
break and when we would come up
with the peak the wind would try to
blow us over and the stern would come
almost straight up and the wave would
break under the tail pushing the nose down
and we the boat, would try surfing but couldn't
surf as fast as the water is racing and thank
God for the cone and its rode, to hold us

214

back from certain disaster. Without it I
think these waves would roll us over
like so much chaff.
Then we would slide backwards to the
bottom and then it looks like the whole
sixty foot wall of water is going to fall
right on top of you, but no. Up we go
like an elevator up to the next wind blown
top. At the bottom all I can see is this
huge wall of water, no sky, just water,
'cause my head is under the dodger and the
clear view is over the stern. Then at
the top all you can see beyond is
row after row of more waves coming
at you and feel the full fury of the
wind, stingingly wet. My twentieth day
out here. Like a roller coaster!!

back from certain disaster. Without it I think these waves would roll us over like so much chaffe.

Then we would slide backwards to the bottom and then it looks like the whole sixty foot wall of water is going to fall right on top of you but no, up we go like an elevator to the next wind blown top. At the bottom all I can see is this huge wall of water, no sky just water, cause my head is under the dodger and the clear view is over the top. Then at the top all you can see beyond is row after row of more waves coming at you and feel the full fury of the wind, stingingly wet. My twentyeth day out here. Like a rollercoaster!!

Friday
8-13-93 4 AM   53:05.21 20:32.91 443 NM C 81°
Have been awake for about thirty min. Made
some coffee. First time in two days am able to
use stove. The winds let off yesterday evening
so that I could get some sleep. Looks like they're
blowing about twenty and the seas have calmed
down to big swells. Spent most of yesterday
just hanging on and trying to brace myself and
with no sleep the night before I feel like a
zombie. I'm taking on water from some place.
The bilge pump comes on and off every
twenty minutes or so and has been all night.
I went around and checked all the through-hull
fittings and they are all closed except engine
intake water but see no leak around pipe,
but did see a trickle under the engine
running forward from aft. So think it's the packing
around the rudder shaft. Can't get to it without emptying out the storage locker under the
seat behind the wheel. It's not a gusher, so
will wait for more day light and calmer conditions
before taking a closer look. Made a hundred miles
in the last thirty-six hours, in the storm. Drove
me back to my rhumb line.

Friday
8-13-93   4:AM   53:05.21   20:32.91 with 443 NM <81°

Have been awake for about thirty min. Made
some coffee, first time in two days am able to
use stove. The winds let off yesterday evening
so that I could get some sleep, looks like there
blowing about twenty and the seas have calmed
down to big swells. Spent most of yesterday
just hanging on and trying to brace myself and
with no sleep the night before I feel like a
zombie. Im taking on water from some place,
the bilge pump comes on and of every
twenty minutes on so and has been all night.
I went around and checked all the through hull
fittings and they are all closed except engine
intake water but see no leak around pipe
but did see a trickle under the engine
running forward from aft. to think its the packing
around the rudder shaft. Can't get to it without emptying out the storage locker under the
seat behind the wheel. Its not a gusher so
will wait for more daylight and calmer conditions
before taking a closer look. Made a hundred miles
in the last thirty six hours, in the storm, drove
me back to my rube line.

12 Noon 8-13   53:15.74   19:57.88   419 mi. to go
Wind shifted back to west-north-west. Sun came
out. On port reach. Wind fifteen to twenty.
Full genoa, reefed main, moving right along.
Emptied out aft and port locker. Found packing
leaking around rudder shaft. I wrapped it with
some T-shirt material saturated with some olive
oil. Cut up a soup can into about a two inch
strip. Put that around the T-shirt material and
held the whole thing in place with two stainless
steel clamps. It stopped the leak, at least
for now. Not an easy task! Not much room
to get two hands on the situation. Cramped space.
Boat rolling, pitching, still under way on it's
own. Probably should have waited for calmer
conditions but what if it gets rougher again?
It's done now. Couldn't have it on my mind any
longer.
7 PM

> At times like a seabird I've danced with grace upon the wind,
> At times the bottlenose would join me and we'd splash the crest as friends,
> And at times the lonely call would whisper in my ear,
> And tons of brine would crack to send shivers down of fear.

Sun came out this afternoon. How wonderful

12 Noon 8-13   53:15.74   19:57.88   419 mi to go

Wind shifted back to ~~west~~ north-west, sun came
out. On port reach, wind fifteen to twenty,
full genoa, reefed main moving right along.
Emptyed out aft and port locker, found packing
leaking around rudder shaft. I wrapped it with
some T-shirt material saturated with some olive
oil, cut up a soup can into about a two inch
strip put that around the T-shirt material and
held the whole thing in place with two stainless
steel clamps. It stopped the leak at least
for now. Not an easy task! Not much room
to get two hands on the situation, cramped space,
boat rolling, pitching, still under way on its
own. Probabally should have waited for calmer
conditions but what if it gets rougher again?
Its done now, couldn't have it on my mind any
longer.
7 PM
   At times like a seabird she danced with
grace upon the wind, at times the bottlenose
would join me and we'd splash the crests
as friends, and at times the lonley call
would wisper in my ear and tones of brine
would crack to send shivers down of fear.
   Sun came out this afternoon. How wonderful

to feel the rays. Clear bright skies, lots of
jet contrails. Little silver specks moving east,
moving west, leaving in their wake ribbons
of clouds which gather together and filter the
rays. Imagine being a part of a tribe of ancient
peoples who have no idea of a jet plane and wonder
what they would think of these silver specks
in the sky making clouds? Silver speck Gods?
11 PM
Just went up to relieve myself over the starboard
side. A dark mysterious night, no moon just
light from the stars filtered through high
wispy clouds

Bioluminescent plankton,
Seemingly suspends me,
As if I am on a magic carpet,
Flying through the near total
Blackness of space.
Illuminated only by their greenish eerie glow,
My water as it splashes,
More brightly do they show.

❀

When the sun sizzles on the pond,
My heart remembers you.
And when it rises at the dawn,
My heart remembers you.
Even when you're far away,
Across the sea so vast and blue,
Or, even on the moon.
Fear not my heart is here to stay,

to feel the rays. Clear bright skys, lots of jet contrails, little silver specks moving east moving west, leaving in their wake ribbons of clouds wich gather together and filter the rays. Imagine being a part of a tribe of ancient peoples who have no idea of a jet plane and won-der what they would think of these silver specks in the sky making clouds? Silver specks Gods?

11:PM

Just went up to releave myself over the starboard side, a dark mysterious night, no moon just light from the stars filtered through high wispy clouds. Bioluminescent plankton, seemingly suspends me as if I am on a magic carpet flying through the near total blackness of space, illumanated only by the greenish erie glow. My water as it splashes, more brightly do they show.

When the sun sizzles on the pond, my heart remembers you, and when it rises at the dawn, my heart remembers you, Evan when your far away, accross the sea so vast and blue or evan on the moon, Fear not my heart is here to stay,

I'll be back to you. . . .soon!

8-14 6:43 AM   53:53.56 18:34.54 360 mi. left
Spent the last half of last night in the cockpit
reading by flash light and dozing off now and then.
Light and gentle winds five to ten. Actually
got to see the sun come up. First time since
leaving Trepassey, I think. The first clear morning
that I remember. Am on a port reach with
full sails flying. Winds out of west north-
west, heading north-easterly.

11 AM

❀

How many more horizons
Might need pass beneath my keel,
Before the sight and touch of you,
My senses do reveal?
Far too many risings to witness till the day
Your voice is heard by these ears,
So very far away.

The wind is petering out.

6 PM   Calm. Wind is gone. Pulled down main
at 3 and rolled up the genoa. Started up the
engine at four in order to make some headway.

I'll be back to you···· soon!

8-14 6:43 AM   53; 53, 54. 18. 34. 54   360 mi LEFT c85°

I spent the last half of last night in the cockpit
reading by flashlight and dosing off now and then.
Light and gentle winds five to ten. Actually
got to see the sun come up, first time since
leaving Trepassey, I think, the first clear morning
that I remember. Am on a port reach with
full sails flying. Winds out of west north-
-west, heading north-easterly

11 AM
        How many more horizons might ~~need~~
need pass beneath my keel, before the
sight and touch of you my senses do
reveal. Far too many risings to witness
till the day, your voice is heard, by these ears,
so very far away.

The wind is petering out. ~~~~~

6 PM Calm. Wind is gone. Pulled down main
at 3 and rolled up the genoa. started up the
engine at four in order to make some headway

224

and charge the batteries. Don't like the noise
much, but better than sitting out here and
not moving. "To be in hell is to drift;
to be in heaven is to steer." George Bernard
Shaw. -   54:07.61   17:58.38   335 NM to go.

11 PM Calm - calm. Motored until now.
Saw a vessel just after dark. Passed
across my bow from starboard to port.
Close about two to three miles. I've
shut down the engine and turned on my
anchor light, which is the white light
on top of the mast. Need to lie down for
some rest.

Sunday morning 6 AM 8-15-93   54:16.39   17:37.05
Three hundred and twenty mi. to the Bloody
Foreland. Only traveled fifteen mi. since last
evening. Another clear morning and clear
sunrise. Woke a few times last night. Got up
to relieve myself and to take a look around.
Eerie silence. Not even a few ripples to
lap against the side. Flat calm. Birds
sitting all around me all night and still
are there this morning. Have been motoring

and charge the batteries. Don't like the noise much but better than sitting out here and not moving. "To be in hell is to drift; to be in heaven is to steer." George Bernard Shaw. — 54:07.61 17:58.38 **335** NM TO GO

11:PM Calm - calm, motored until now. Saw a ~~tell~~ vessel just after dark, passed across my bow from starboard to port, close, ~~about~~ about two to three miles. I've shut down the engine and turned on my anchor light, which is the white lite on top of the mast. Need to lye down for some rest.

Sunday morning 6AM 8-15-93 59:16.39 17:37.05 three hundred and twenty mi to the ~~Pretty~~ Bloody Forland, only traveled fifteen mi since last evening. Another clear morning and clear sunrise, woke a few times last night, got up to relieve myself and to take a look around. Eire silence, not even a few ripples to lap against the side, flat calm, birds sitting all around me all night and still are there this morning. Have been motoring

226

since about four. Stopped for breakfast. Oatmeal,
raisins, maple syrup, milk (made
from powdered), coffee (black). I make coffee
in a pan, (cowboy coffee). Boil water, sprinkle
in coffee, stir, let settle one minute, pour
into thermos. Most grounds stay in pan.
This is the first really calm day I've experienced.
It's a mill pond out here. No sign
of any ripples anywhere to the horizon
three hundred and sixty degrees all around.
This whole circle of the planet, as far as I
can see, is all mine; well, me and the birds.

2 PM   8-1-93 54:23.59 16:58.38   calm -
Made about twenty four mi. since 6 AM.
Motoring on flat calm seas. No wind. Sunshine,
like summer day. Naked as a jay bird, soaking
up the rays. The only ripples on the pond
from my wake. The thoughts of jumping overboard
for a swim are almost overwhelming.
The vastness of the water seemingly
trying to convince me to come on in.
I see on the chart that my position is
close to where the sea floor rises from
thirteen hundred fathoms up to six hundred

since about four, stopped for breakfast, oatmeal, raisins, maple syrup, milk (made from powdered) coffee (black). I make coffee in a pan, (cowboy coffee) boil water, sprinkle in coffee, stir, let settle one minute, pour into thermous, most grounds stay in pan. This is the first really calm day I've experienced, it's a millpond out here, no sign of any ripples anywhere to the horizon three hundred and sixty degrees all around. This whole circle of the planet, as far as I can see, is all mine, well, me and the birds.

2 PM 8-15-93   54,23.59   16:58.38   Calm —
Made about twenty four mi. since 6 AM motoring on flat calm seas, no wind, sunshine, like summer day, naked as a jay bird, soaking up the rays. The only ripples on the pond from my wake. The thoughts of jumping overboard for a swim are almost overwhelming. The vastness of the water seemingly trying to convince me to come on in. I see on the chart that my position is close to where the sea floor rises from thirteen hundred fathoms up to six hundred

228

and forty, (a fathom is six feet). I did the math.
Thirteen hundred fathoms is seventy-eight hundred
feet (that's deeper than Mt. Washington in New
Hampshire which is about six thousand feet above
sea level). Almost eight thousand feet of water
calling me to take the plunge.
 I decided to stay on board and douse myself
with a couple of buckets full instead. I feel
like a big chicken so guess I have to
live with it.
 Around noontime while motoring along I
crossed through a line of plastic trash.
Like a ribbon floating, a ribbon of plastic
about five to ten feet wide all lined up
together that stretched as far as I could
see north and south of me. Really strange,
like it all had an affinity for itself, staying
together like that. I wondered if it was American
trash being pushed along by winds and currents
and felt bad a the prospects of American trash
littering up beaches across the ocean.

8 PM 8-15-93 Still calm. Not a bit of breeze. Hot day,
in the eighties, my guess. Feels so good
to be clean!! Soaped up and rinsed off

and forty, (a fathom is six feet). I did the math, thirteen hundred fathoms is seventy eight hundred feet (thats deeper than Mt. Washington in New Hampshire which is about six thousand feet above sea level. Almost eight thousand feet of water calling me to take the plunge.

I decide to stay on board and douse myself with a couple of buckets full instead. I feel like a big chicken so you guess I have to live with it.

Around noontime while motoring along I crossed through a line of plastic trash. Like a ribbon floating, a ribbon of plastic about five to ten feet wide all lined up together that streached as far as I could see north and south of me. Really strange, like it all had an afinity for itself, staying together like that. I wondered if it was American trash being pushed along by winds and currents and felt bad at the prospects of American trash littering up beaches across the Ocean.

8:pm 8-15-93 Still calm, not a bit of breeze, hot day, in the eightys my guess. Feels so good to be clean!! Soaped up and rinsed off

230

with fresh water. First real bath-shower
since the third, twelve days
ago. This is the end of the twenty-third
day. ～～～

> Tonight let me be a young man,
> And dream young men's dreams,
> Of being held, of being loved,
> Caressed, how real it seems.
> Of touching and of tasting,
> Lips where musky odors dwell,
> Of throbbing and of wanting,
> The throbbing there to stay a spell.
> Of entering and of leaving,
> Of flickering candlelight,
> Reflecting from within the eyes,
> Of her that holds me in delight.
> Let me feel and be a part,
> As spasms overtake,
> Let me feel the warmth of her,
> In the morning as I wake.
> And let me as I turn the page,
> When evenings light takes flight,
> Remember her with loving,
> As our hair turns white.

Starry, starry night.

8-16-93 6:30 AM   54:34.10   16:37.70   283 NM
to Bloody
Foreland

There are slight ripples on the surface
here and there like a patch work as far
as I can see all around. The sun came up
on a clear horizon but behind me to

231

with fresh water, first real bath-shower ~~since the third~~ since the third, twelve days ago. This is the end of the twenty third day.

Tonite let me be a young man, And dream young mens dreams, Of being held of being loved, Caressed, how real it seems. Of touching and of tasting, Lips where musky odors dwell, Of throbing and of wanting, The throbing there to stay a spell. Of entering and leaving, Of flickering candle light, Reflecting from within the eyes, Of her that holds me in delight. Let me feel, and be a part, as spasoms oortake, Let me feel the warmpth af her, in the morning as I wake. And let me as I turn the page, When evenings light takes flight, Remember her with loving, As our hair turns white.
Starry, starry night.

8-16-93 6:30AM   54:34.10 16:37.20 283 N.M. TO BLUFF POLEIRINTO

There are slight ripples on the surface here and there like a patchwork as far as I can see all around. the sun came up on a clear horizon but behind me to

the west-south-west clouds are gathering
on that horizon. Over head a few clouds
and a few jet contrails. It's Monday
morning. I imagine people getting up in
Europe or London and flying over
to Boston, New York, Chicago for breakfast.
I'm Motoring along. Pretty boring. Pressing
onward. Scotland or Bust!

8-16-93 6 PM   54:45.98   15:21.08 237 NM to Ireland
End of twenty-fourth day out here. I figure
another four or five days to Ireland and
Jim and Marilyn leave to go home in
eight days, on the twenty-fourth. Around
noon today the wind picked up enough to
hoist the main and the genoa and sail
wing and wing all afternoon. I filled the
fuel tank before that. It took three gallons
out of one of my two five gallon spare jerry
cans. I probably motored about twenty hours
since leaving Trepassey. The winds picked
up steadily all afternoon and now are blowing
about twenty and the seas are six to ten and
I expect a rough night. I hope not a too rough
night!

the west south-west clouds are gathering
on that horizon. Over head a few clouds
and a few jet contrails. Its Monday
morning. I imagine people getting up in
~~Europe~~ Europe or London and flying over
to Boston, New York, Chicago for breakfast.
I'm motoring along. Pretty boring. Pressing
onward, Scotland or Bust!

8-16-93 6:PM   54:45.98 15:21.08 237 N.M. (C 800 M)
                                    TO IRELAND
End of twenty fourth day out here. I figure
another four or five days to Ireland and
Jim and Marilyn leave to go home in
eight days, on the twenty fourth. Around
noon today the wind picked up enough to
hoist the main and the genoa and sail
wing and wing all afternoon. I filled the
fuel tank before that, it took three gallons
out of one of my two five gallon spare jerry
cans. I probably motored about twenty hours
since leaving Trepassey. The winds picked
up steadily all afternoon and now are blowing
about twenty and the seas are six to ten and
I expect a rough night. I hope not a tough
night!

234

Oft' before the storm arrives,
The stars seem falling from the skies.
And, morning mists refracting beams to show,
The coming waves as all aglow.

Then the evenings ominous shadows,
Of cavernous canyons in row after row,
With peak after peak spraying wet blow.

A line of three fourth's braided rode,
With cone of canvas off her tail,
A hundred feet stretched taut across,
Ten fathoms down the swale.

Streaks of white lace each face,
Rolling with colossal grace,
Tossing her as if to waste,
With a roaring sound.
Lines against the bare pole,
Ever slapping on my mind,
The gimbaled light flickers,
And leaves me to my fright,
On the mid-ships cabin sole,
Waiting for the final,
throughout what seems,
Endless night.

8-16-93 9 PM

"And down with the sun goes the breeze,
That put the ripples on the bay,
And carried me in it's arms,
And rocked me through the day.
Now it blows hard and cold,
I bundle for a night of bold,
Feel a tenseness in my grip,
Set out the rode and canvas cone,

Oft before the storm arrives, the stars
seen falling from the skys, and morning
mists refracting beams to show, the coming
waves as all aglow. Then the evenings ominous
shadows, of cavernish canyons in rows after
rows, with peak after peak, spraying wet blow.
A line of three fourth's braided rode, with
cone of canvas off her tail, a hundred feet streaks
taught accross, ten fathoms down the swale.
Streaks of white lace each face, rolling with
colosal grace, tossing her, as if to waste,
with a roaring sound.
Lines against the bare pole ever slapping
on my mind, the gimbled light flickers and
leaves me to my fright, on the mid ships
cabin sole, waiting for the final, throughout
what seems, endless night.

8-16-93   9:PM
"And down with the sun goes the breeze,
that put the ripples on the bay, and carried
me in its ~~over~~ arms, and rocked me through
the day. Now it blows hard and cold I
bundle for a night of bold, feel a tenseness
in my grip, set out the rode and canvis cone,

236

That might well save my little ship."

8-17 6 AM   54:52 61   13:47.20   #4 182 NM
A very stormy night. Large seaways to fifty
feet as a guess. Fifty to sixty knot winds
after midnight and now starting to abate
but still blowing at least forty and steady.
Nothing like the blow last week. Looking
back I now feel that storm was as close
to hurricane force as you can get without
any doubts by me. I think the eye of it passed
to my south and east, I will not soon forget
the experience of it. This storm was certainly
a full gale and now still gale force while
diminishing. Made good time with the blow
about fifty knots during the night. Less than
two hundred to way point # (no.) four just off the
Bloody Foreland, wonder what it's like there and
why the name?
8-17   Noon   54:54.80   13.04.62   #4 158 NM C 90°
Winds have come way off. Genoa - full and
motoring. Thirty-four mi. since this morning. That's
about five knots per hour and about top
speed for this hull size.
8-17 6 PM   54:56.42   12:20.91   WP#4 133 NM C 88°
Twenty more mi. this afternoon. Getting antsy

that might well save my little ship".

8-17 6AM   54.52.61 13.47.20 ᵗ4 182 N.M.

A very stormy night, large seaways to fifty
feet as a guess, fifty to sixty knot winds
after midnight and now starting to abate
but still blowing at least forty and steady.
Nothing like the blow last week. Looking
back I now feel that storm was as close
to hurricane force as you can get without
any doubts by me. I think the eye of it passed
to my south and east, I will not soon forget
the experiance of it. This storm was certainly a full gale and now still gale force while
diminishing. Made good time with the blow
about fifty knots during the night. Less than
two hundred to way point # four just off the
Bloody Farland, wonder what its like there and
why the name?

8-17 noon   54.54.80 13.04.62 ᵗ4 158 N.M.
                                          c. 90°
Winds have come way off. Genoa-full and
motoring. thirty four mi since this morning thats
~~about~~ about five knts. per hour and about top
speed for this hull size.

8-17 6PM.   54.56.42 12.20.91 WP #4
                                        133 NM c 88°
twenty more mi. this afternoon. Getting antsy

you know anxious, about being so close to land.
The wind seems to be holding about twenty
knots, motor sailing with full genoa, wheel tied
off with a little port weather helm, wind coming
over the port aft rail out of the west-north-west
enough off of the stern to squeak out a
nice reach. I cross my fingers and toes
hoping it to last all night.

❀

Once upon a moon lit tide,
I set my sails and tried to hide.
Out beyond the furtherest shelf,
Where fears begin was found myself.
Beyond the smell of musty earth,
In-raging seas,
Began re-birth.

8-18-93 6 AM   54:56.65 10.41.28 WP#4 77 NM C 82°
The wind held steady for most of the night.
Enough to make fifty six more miles!!
Rolled up the genoa and am motoring.
The wind is not enough to keep the sail full
and it was just flapping around. Have the
motor at almost full throttle, not concerned
about running out of fuel this close to land.
What I am concerned about is another storm

you know anxious, about being so close to land.
The wind seems to be holding ~~of~~ about twenty
knots. motor sailing with full genoa, wheel tied
off with a little port ~~the weather~~ helm, wind coming
over the port aft rail out of the west-north-west
enough off of the steam to squeak out a
nice reach. I cross my fingers and toes
hopeing it to last all night.

Once upon a moon ~~tide~~ lit tide, I set my sails
and tried to hide.
Out beyond the furthest shelf, where fears
begin was found myself.
~~Beyond~~ and the smell of musty earth, in raging
seas, began re-birth.

8-18-93 6AM   54:56.65   10.41.28   WPT 9   C 82°
                                           77 NM
The wind held steady for most of the night.
Enough to make fifty six more miles!!
Rolled up the genoa and am motoring.
The wind is not enough to keep the sail full
and it was just flapping around. Have the
motor at almost full throttle, not concerned
about running out of fuel this close to land.
What I am concerned about is another storm

242

coming along when I'm this close to a rocky, uncharted (I don't have a chart) shore after all of this don't want to end up smashed against some rocks.

8-18 6 PM   55:04.42   09:28.08

Motored all day. Pretty calm. About one in the afternoon spotted a large fishing boat off of the starboard bow about ten degrees and on the horizon. Three hours later I came close enough along side to converse loudly with the captain. He asked if I was the Kandahar, as they and other boats have been on the look out for me for about a week. I would say she, the boat, was about eighty feet or so, and they were hauling up large crab traps. I said that I was the Kandahar and looking for a good harbor but don't have a chart. The Capt. pointed off to the east, and I took a bearing in the direction he was pointing, thanked him and headed off in that direction. He said he would call the Coast Guard and report seeing me. I'm about thirty miles off the coast and the only hint of land is the cloud bank that is hanging above it.

comaining along when Im this close to a rocky, uncharted, (I don't have a chart) shore after all of this don't want to end up smashed against some rocks.

8-18- 6 P.M.   55:04.42 09:28.08

Motored all day, pretty calm. About one in the afternoon spotted a large fishing boat off of the starboard bow about ten degrees and on the horizon. Three hours later I came close enough alongside to converse loudly with the captain. He asked if I was the Kandahar as they and other boats have been on the lookout for me for about a week. I would say she, the boat, was about eighty feet or so and they were hauling up large crab traps. I said that I was the Kandahar and looking for a good harbor but don't have a chart. The Capt. pointed off to the east and I took a bearing in the direction he was pointing, thanked him and headed off in that direction. He said he would call the coast guard and report seeing me.

I'm about thirty miles off the coast and the only hint of land is the cloud bank that is hanging above it.

8-18   8:30 PM   55:07 09:10
Saw a light reflecting off of a darkening
sky and headed in that direction. Took a
compass bearing.
8-18   10:30   55:06   08:56
Followed the light for hours to the
point where it lay just over the horizon
where I can see the actual light source
and not just a reflection against a darkly
clouded sky. The one in the middle of
now three flashing lights; one ten-points
port off the bow, and one ten-points starboard
off the bow, is the brightest and it's the
one I am going into or, heading for. I figure
about thirty miles away.
It's a cool-cold, damp night, like seems all
of the nights out here are cool-cold, damp,
lonely...
8-19 3 AM   Slept a few hours in the
cockpit. Now up and making coffee. It's eerie
out here tonight. Dark clouds about, but
stars are visible through breaks in the
cover. Black space speckled with stars
gleaming as diamonds. Glistening pure white.
And then the light from distant shore sweeping

8-18   8:30 PM   53.07 — 09:10 —

Saw a light reflecting off of a darkening
sky and headed in that direction. Took a
compass bearing.

8-18   10:30   55:06   08:56

Followed the light for hours to the
point where it lay just over the horizon
where I can see the actual light source
and not just a reflection against a darkly
clouded sky. The one in the middle of
now three flashing lights, one ten points
port of the bow and one ten points starboard
of the bow, is the brightest and its the
one I am going into, heading for, I figure
about thirty miles away.

It's a cool-cold damp night, like seems all
of the nights out here are cool-cold, damp,
lonely....

8-19   3AM Slept a few hours in the
cockpit, now up and making coffee. Its eerie
out here tonight. Dark clouds about but
stars are visible through breaks in the
cover, black space speckeled with stars
gleaming as diamonds, glisining pure white.
And then the light from distant shore sweeping

246

the heavens as a musical score. I'm beginning
to feel the excitement of being able to call her
in a few hours and exclaiming my love and
devotion to her for being there in my life.
A long, gentle, rolling seaway with wind blown
foam remaining from the storm of two days ago

❀

Smeared and streaked by the wind,
illuminated by the reflection of the beacon,
into wonderful and grotesque features,
as I stand on the rail and let nature prevail,
cold and stiff from holding my pee,
pee to sea, foam to foam, carry this message home.
I'm well and my heart feels swell,
for land lies near just beyond,
just beyond, just beyond, there. "Do you hear me? "
I yell, "My heart feels swell.

What a splendid night! Now I just have to
make it to shore, to a harbor, to a phone!

8-19-93   12:30 PM   Burton Port, Ireland.
I tied up to the pier here about eleven. The harbormaster
told me to stay aboard or at least around the
area, the customs man will be right along. He
was here within thirty minutes and we sat in
the cockpit while he asked me some questions and
looked over my passport. I suddenly got very nervous
as I remembered a joint that one of my friends

the heavens as a musical score. I'm beginning to feel the excitment of being able to call her in a few hours and exclaiming my love and devotion to her for being there in my life. A long, gentel, rolling seaway with wind blown foam remaining from the storm of two days ago, smeared and streaked by the wind, illuminated by the reflection of the beacon, into wonderful and grotesk features, as I stand on the rail and let nature prevail cold and stiff from holding my pee, pee to sea, foam to foam carry this message home, I'm well and my heart feels swell, for land lyes near just beyond, just beyond, jest beyond there, "do you hear me", I yell, "my heart feels swell". What a splendid night! Now I just have to make it to shore, to a harbor, to a phone!

8-19-93 12:30PM Burton Port, Ireland.
I tied up to the pier here about eleven. The harbor-master told me to stay aboard or at least around the area, the customs man will be right along. He was here within thirty minutes and we sat in the cockpit while he asked me some questions and looked over my passport. I suddenly got very nervous as I remembered a joint that one of my friends

Arranmore Island
First Landfall – IRELAND

WRH 2012

250

gave me back in Plymouth at the dock before I
left. I had put it in the finger of a glove and
forgotten it until then, but the customs guy
didn't even go down below to look around. In
twenty minutes he was gone and said enjoy your
trip as he departed.

The harbormaster helped me with the pay phone
and I called Margi first thing, but got her
answering machine and left a message about
where I am and would call her again later.
Then called my father and asked him to let
everyone else know that I'm alright. Now
going to walk up the hill to town and look for a
hamburger!

6 PM Back on board

No hamburger, but a nice piece of steak at the
first pub on the right side of the road and
two beers also, on the house. I'm a little
woozy, not being much of a drinker. Everyone
there full of fun and conversation, most of
which went right over my head. The English
language yes, but what were they saying?

A large fishing vessel came in a while I was in
the pub, eighty feet I would guess and lots
of commotion on the pier. Japanese fish

gave me back in Plymouth at the dock, before I left. I had put it in the finger of a glove and forgotten it until then but the customs guy didn't even go down below to look around, in twenty minutes he was gone and said enjoy your trip as he departed.

The harbormaster helped me with the payphone and I called Margie first thing but got her answering machine and left a message about where I am and would call her again later. Then called my father and asked him to let everyone else know that I'm alright. Now going to walk up the hill to town and look for a hamburger!

6 PM Back on board.

No hamburger but a nice piece of steak at the first pub on the right side of the road and two beers also, on the house, I'm a little woosey, not being much of a drinker. Every-one there full of fun and conversation, most of which went right over my head, the English language yes but what were they saying? A large fishing vessel came in while I was in the pub, eighty feet I would guess and lots of commotion on the pier. Japanese fish

252

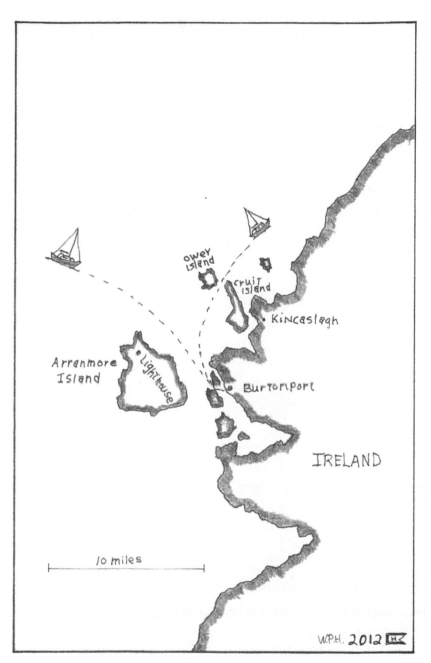

Ower
Island

cruit
island

Kincaslagh

Arranmore
Island

Lighthouse

Burtonport

IRELAND

10 miles

W.P.H. 2012

buyers here to purchase the best of the
catch. Every woman (looked like), in town
dressed in white with white netting on their
heads, and quite a few men also appeared
in the streets. They proceeded to the fish
processing plant, along with a steady stream of fork
lifts conveying the catch from ship to plant
in large insulated boxes.
9 PM
I got to talking with a local fisherman about
the best way to get out of here in the morning
and make my way along the coast (The Bloody
Foreland). He drove me to his house a few
miles away, where I got to meet his wife and
two daughters, and picked up a chart of the coast,
which he gave me.

8-20-93   12:30
Passing off of the Bloody Foreland,
rocks everywhere. Like skeletons left
after massive storms that eons of massive
waves have left after washing all the soil
away for miles off the coast. Outcroppings
of ledge exposed to the relentless rhythms

255

buyers here to purchase the best of the
catch. Every woman (looks like) in town
dressed in white with white netting on their
heads and quite a few men also appeared
in the streets and proceded to the fish
processing plant and a steady stream of fork
lifts conveying the catch from ship to plant
in large insulated boxes.
9 PM
        I got to talking with a local fisherman about
    the best way to get out of here in the morning
    and make my way along the coast (the Bloody
Foreland) and he drove me to his house a few
miles away, where I got to meet his wife and
two daughters and pick up a chart of the coast,
which he gave me.

    8-20-93   12:30
Passing off of the Bloody Foreland,
rocks everywhere, like skeletons left
after massive storms with eons of massive
waves have left after washing all of the soil
away far miles of the coast. Outcroppings
of ledge exposed to the relentless rythoms

256

of white-capped rollers
stealing a piece of Ireland with every
succession of storms.
Left Burton Port at 9:30 and skirted
between Owey and Cruit Islands. Many
silhouettes of stone structures, telling tales
of long ago. Standing as a testament to
hardy souls who lived here once upon
a time.
Heading for Portmore or beyond, depends
on weather. It's blowing fifteen to twenty
and the seaway is running with me.
Motor sailing with the main out over the
starboard side, wind over the port rear
quarter, moving right along. I'm in
the cockpit on the port seat with the wheel
between my knees.
Portmore lies just beyond Malin Head,
which is the most northern part of Ireland.

8-21-93
It's about 3:30 PM. I'm about two or three
miles off of the Mull of Kintyre and have
been here for a few hours. At the wheel
with the engine at full throttle, no sails.

of ~~crisp~~ white capped rollers
stealing a piece of Ireland with every ~~succession~~
~~successful blow.~~ succession of storms.
Left Burton Port at 9:30 and skirted
between Owey and Cruit islands. Many
silouettes of stone structures, telling tales
of long ago. Standing as a testiment to
hardy souls who lived here once upon
a time.
Heading for Portmore or beyond, depends
on weather. It's blowing fifteen to twenty
and the seaway is running with me.
Motor sailing with the main out over the
starboard side, wind over the port rear
quarter, moving right along. I'm in
the cockpit on the port seat with the wheel
between my knees.
Portmore lies just beyond Malin Head
which is the most northern part of Ireland.

8-21-93
It's about 3:30 P.M. I'm about two or three
miles off of the Mull of Kintyre and have
been here for a few hours. At the wheel
with the engine at full throttle, no sails.

258

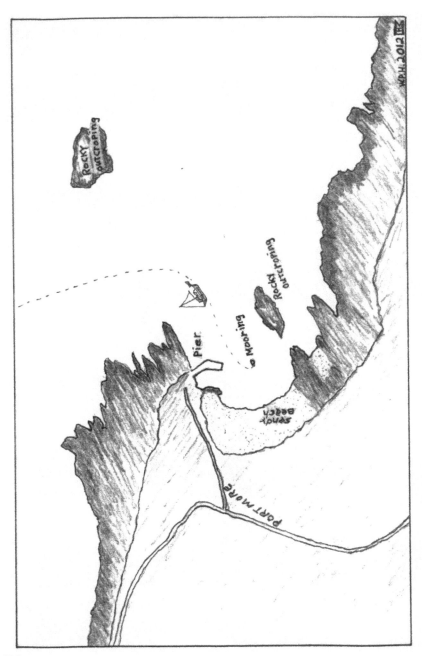

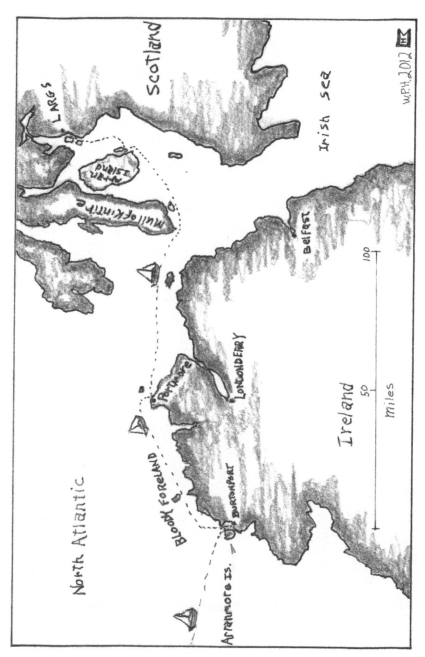

Kintyre rises out of the sea like a
mountain with sheer rock faces to my
left, (port). I've been looking at the same
rocks now for hours waiting for the
tide to change. The whole Irish sea is
emptying out into the North Atlantic through
this narrow channel of about twelve to fifteen
miles wide. If the engine quits the current
will push me back out to sea in no
time. Left Portmore at six-thirty this
morning with the fishing fleet there, about
five boats. Arrived there just as the sun
was going down last evening, thank God
for the chart I was given in Burton Port.
After I arrived and tied up to a mooring
that was offered, one of the fishermen let me
use his phone and I called Margi.
Its been twenty-nine days since last we talked
and it doesn't sound good. Well, I mean she sounded
different, distant. Said she wasn't coming
over. She needed to be there, and something about
getting on with her life and would see me when
I came back. There's a knot in my stomach.

Kintyre rises out of the sea like a mountain with sheer rock faces to my left, (port), I've been looking at the same rocks now for hours waiting for the tide to change, the whole Irish sea is emptying out into the North Atlantic through this narrow channel of about twelve to fifteen miles wide, if the engine quits the current will push me back out to sea in no time. Left Portmore at six thirty this morning with the fishing fleet there, about five boats. Arrived there just as the sun was going down last evening, thank God for the chart I was given in Burton Port. After I arrived and tied up to a mooring that was offered, one of the fishermen let me use his phone and I called Margie. Its been twenty nine days since last we talked and it doesn't sound good, well I mean she sounded different, distant, said she wasn't comming over, she needed to be there and something about getting on with her life and would see me when I came back, there's a knot in my stomach.

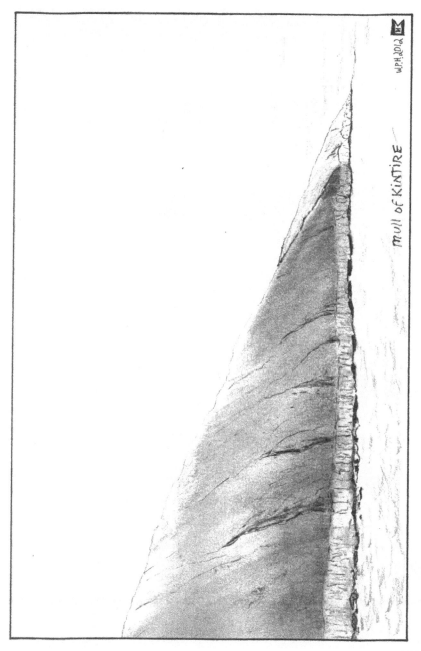

mull of Kintire

W.P.H. 2012

Sunday 8-22 12:30 AM I've picked up
a mooring in a harbor on the east
side of Arran Island. It's ghostly
quiet. I'm only about fifty yards off of shore.
There's a smaller island with a high
hill silhouetted against the sky. Holy
Island, a few lights here and there can
be seen, bright spots against its darkness.
Quite a few lights on Arran Island,
A small town on the distant shore with
even more lights, allowed me to see my
way into the harbor fairly well, even though
it's a dark night. Eighteen hours from
Malin Head - Portmore, but five of those
were spent in the same spot off the Mull
of Kintyre waiting for the tide to slacken
off so I could make some headway.
I'm guessing only five or six hours
to go to make Largs and the end of my
journey. Need some rest from the wheel but
am not sleepy. Still feel a bit wired from
the strains of the day. The quiet and the calm
are disturbing, not used to it.

Sunday 8-22 12:30 AM. I've picked up
a ~~mooring~~ mooring in a harbor on the east
side of Arran Island. It's ~~quite~~ ghastly
quiet, I'm only about fifty yards off of shore.
There's a smaller island with a high
hill silouetted against the sky, Holy
Island, a few lights here and there can
be seen, bright spots against it's dark-
-ness. Quite a few lights on Arran Island,
a small town on the distant shore with
even more lights, allowed me to see my
way into the harbor fairly well even though
it's a dark night. Eighteen hours from ~~Malin~~
Malin Head - Portmore, but five of those
were spent in the same spot off the Mull
of Kintyre waiting for the tide to slacken
off so I could make some headway.
    I'm guessing only five or six hours
to go to make Largs and the end of my
journey. Need some rest from the wheel but
am not sleepy, still feel a bit wired from
the strains of the day. The quiet and the calm
are disturbing, not used to it.

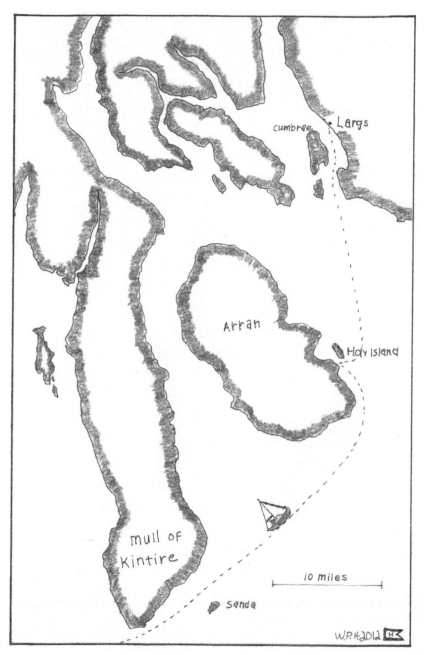

Largs

Cumbrae

Arran

Holy Island

Mull of Kintire

Sanda

10 miles

W.P.H.2012

Monday 8-23   20 Lindsay Crescent, Largs
In the living room of Jim's dad, on
the couch where I slept last night, it's eight
thirty a.m. Have been up awake for at least
an hour and a half reading love letters from
Margi that Jim and Marilyn brought over
for me. Two large manila envelopes full of
letters, and another cassette tape of selected
love songs put together by her, titled "More
bud hits for the sea". So many thoughts
of her in my head, tears of happiness flow
and ebb, choked with emotion.
 I arrived yesterday at about two thirty in the
afternoon and picked up a mooring close to
shore and down town Largs in the famous
Firth of Clyde. In my haste of getting ashore
I let the painter (the line on my dingy) slip
out of my hands and it (the dingy) began
to head back out to sea with the current,
which was running at a good clip. Fortunately
two men in a power launch saw my
predicament and went off in pursuit and
returned it to me in a matter of minutes.
After rowing ashore and calling Jim, I
broke into tears at the sight of him
and embraced him with all of my might.

Monday 8-23   20 Lindsay Crescent, Largs
In the living room of Jim's dad's on
the couch where I slept last night. It's eight
thirty a.m. Have been up awake for at least
an hour and a half reading love letters from
Margie that Jim and Marilyn brought over
for me. Two large manila envelopes full of
letters and another cassette tape of selected
love songs put together by her, titled "more
bud hits for the sea". So many thoughts
of her in my head, tears of happiness flow
and ebb, choked with emotion.
    I arrived yesterday at about two thirty in the
afternoon and picked up a mooring close to
shore and downtown Largs in the famous
Firth of Clyde. In my haste of getting ashore
I let the painter (the line on my dingy) slip
out of my hands and it (the dingy) began
to head back out to sea with the current,
which was running at a good clip. Fortunately two men in a power launch saw my
perdicament and went off in persuit and
returned it to me in a matter of minutes.
and after rowing ashore and calling Jim I
broke into tears at the sight of him
and embraced him with all of my might.

270

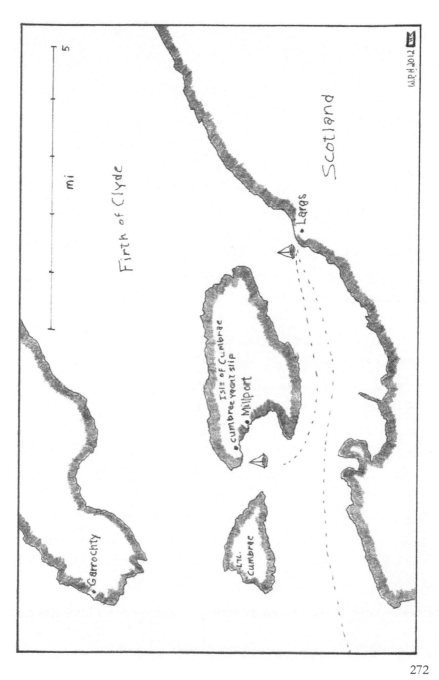

Firth of Clyde

Scotland

Largs

Isle of Cumbrae

cumbree yacht slip

Millport

Ltl. Cumbrae

Garrochty

mi

5

WPHolz 2012

9 AM

Everyone's up now, Jim, his father Jim (Dad) and Marilyn.
Jim went down the street for a loaf of bread.
Yesterday after meeting with everyone, it was
suggested that I would be better off moving
Kandahar to a slip at the yacht basin,
which I did as a matter of safety, seeing
that the mooring in the Clyde that I
had tied up to initially belonged
to someone else, and who knows what it
was really like under water. The wind and currents
here could spell disaster for her and me.
At the yacht basin was a large sheet hanging
with the message "Welcome Bill and Congrat-
ulations". After securing Kandahar, it was supper
time with some of Jim's kin. After that
it was off to the Free Masons Lodge for
celebrating, where I drank too many pints
of ale and met everyone in the place.
Today is Jim's, Marilyn's and their three
daughters' last day in Scotland. They fly out
tomorrow. The local newspaper wants to take
some pictures and ask some questions of me for
a story at eleven this morning at the yacht
basin.

9 AM

Everyone's up now, Jim, his father Jim (DAD) and Marilyn.
Jim went down the street for a loaf of bread.
Yesterday after meeting with everyone it was
suggested that I would be better off mooring
Kandahar to a slip at the yacht basin
which I did as a matter of safety seeing
that the mooring in the Clyde that I
had tied up to initially ~~that probably~~ belonged
to someone else and who knows what it
was really ~~like~~ underwater and the wind and currents
here could spell disaster for her and me.
At the yacht basin was a large sheet hanging
with the message "welcome Bill and congrad-
-ulations". After securing Kandahar it was supper
time with some of Jims kin and after that
it was off to the Free Masons Lodge for
celebrating, where I drank too many pints
of ale and met everyone in the place.
Today is Jim and Marilyn and their three
daughters last day in Scotland they fly out
tomorrow. The local newspaper wants to take
some pictures and ask some questions of me for
a story at eleven this morning at the yacht
basin.

8-24-93 10 PM   20 Lindsay Crescent, Largs, Scotland
Jim, Marilyn and their three daughters left for
home this afternoon. Jim took his largest suitcase
filled with loaves of bread, and among his
clothing three bottles of single malt scotch in another.
Before heading to Glasgow Airport he handed me
thirteen-hundred dollar bills. Money he had owed
me from a vinyl siding job I helped him
with back home before I left, which he had finished
alone, and been paid for. A good thing too, for
I had spent all but fifty of the eight thousand
that I had when the idea of sailing over
here jelled in my mind. A mind full of jello.
I'm sure that's what some might think
about the whole idea. And perhaps so, for some of
those days out there I thought it also.
Will go down and buy a plane ticket home
tomorrow. Jim senior said I may stay as long
as I like so I think I would like to see some
of Scotland while here. Since Margret is not
coming over now, which is my biggest disappointment,
got to do it on my own.

8-27-93 9 PM Yesterday Jim's dad and I motored
across the Clyde to the island of Cumbrae
where we had lunch and met with Stewart

8-24-93 10:PM 20 Lindsay Crescent, Large, Scotland

Jim, Marilyn and their three daughters left for home this afternoon. Jim took his largest suit-case filled with loaves of bread and among his clothing three bottles of single malt scotch in another. Before heading to Glasgo airport he handed me thirteen hundred dollar bills, money he had owed me from a signal siding job I had helped him with back home before I left, which he had finished alone and been paid for. A good thing too, for I had spent all but fifty of the eight thousand that I had had when the idea of sailing over here jelled in my mind. A mind full of jello, I'm sure thats what some might think about the whole idea and perhaps so, some of those days out there I thought it also.

Will go down and buy a plane ticket home tomorrow. Jim senior said I may stay as long as I like and I think I would like to see some of Scotland while here and since Margret is not comming over now, which is my biggest dis--apointment, got to do it on my own.

8-27-93 9:PM Yesterday Jims Dad and I motored across the Clyde to the island of Cumbrae where we had lunch and met with Stewart

276

McIntyre, the owner of Cumbrae Yacht Slip,
and arranged to have Kandahar hauled out
and stored for the winter. I left Kandahar
on a mooring in Millport and turned the
keys over to Stewart, after rowing out to her
with him to point out a few things like
the compression release lever on the Yanmar
one banger, then Jim and I headed back to
the mainland (Largs) on the ferry. Stewart
will haul her out tonight at ten o'clock when
the tide is high, and he doesn't allow owners
to be present at launchings or haulings.
Bought a round trip ticket to Boston
on Wednesday for six-hundred dollars, will
leave for home in two weeks on Sept. ninth.

Your love's a lovely bonus,
To a life that's free and full.
A bonus that has been felt throughout,
Lonely days of damp and chill.
Though storms be ever present,
They'll slip beneath my keel,
Harmless, for I know of love,
And know 'tis I that makes it false,
or makes it real.
Wm.

Mcintyre the owner of Cumbrae Yacht Slip, and aranged to have Kandahar hauled out and stored for the winter. I left Kandahar on a mooring in Millport and turned the keys over to Stewart after rowing out to her with him to point out a few things like the compression release lever on the Yanmar one banger then Jim and I headed back to the mainland (Large) on the ferry. Stewart will haul her out tonight at ten oclock when the tide is high and he doesn't allow owners to be present at launchings or haulings.

Bought a round trip ticket to Boston on Wednesday for six hundred dollars, will leave for home in two weeks on Sept. nineth.

Your love is a lovely bonus, to a life thats free and full.
A bonus that has been felt, through-out, lonely days of damps and chill.
Though storms be ever present, they'll slip beneath my keel, harm less, for I know of love, and know tis I, that makes it false, or makes it real.

Wm.

278

Cumbrae Yacht Slip

Proprietor; WILLIAM S. McINTYRE

STEWART

V.A.T. Reg. No. 265 0853 53

Mr William Howland.

9/6/94

West Bay Road
Millport
Isle of Cumbrae
Tel: 0475 530 566
all 44

Your boat/yacht "...KANDAHAR......" Length 31 ft. is presently stored at Cumbrae Yacht Slip for Winter 1993/4. Your account for slipping, storage and launching for Winter 93/94 is £ 10.00 per ft. length plus V.A.T., half being due now and half 14 days prior to launching when an official V.A.T. receipt will be issued.

Slipping, Storage and Launching	310	00
Towing to and from yard		
Dismantling and topping mast		
Hire of moorings		
Mooring fee .... season		
Lifting and laying moorings		
Antifoul		
Labour		
AD. HERALD. 12/5/94	16	45
" " 27/5/94	16	45
" " 3/6/94	16	45
BOAT ELECTRICS INVOICE N° 93 726	26	44
ARTHUR DUTHIE INVOICE N° 55977	39	36
TOTAL	425	19
V.A.T.	74	40
TOTAL	499	59 = 760.

Received 500 Dollars. =

328 . 78
£170 . 81

All work carried out and the handling of boats solely at owners own liability.

Cumbrae Yacht Slip, Isle of Cumbrae,
Firth of Clide, Scotland.

W.P.H. 2012

Wed. Sept 8   Largs, Scotland
Returned to Largs yesterday, late afternoon.
Went for a train ride up north to find Findhorn,
and Findhorn Park, the intentional community there.
As the train was pulling out of one of the
stations after Largs, a newly boarded passenger
(a young man about twenty), while passing by
my seat, stopped for a moment and began to
have a seizure. I immediately got up, and as he
began to fall, guided him gently to the
floor and held him. One of the passengers in
the forward part of the car (a nurse as it turned
out) came down the isle to assist me and
held his legs down, as he was flailing about
a bit. Then a doctor, who was in the next
forward car showed up. Soon the young
man was over the seizure, and we helped
him up to a seat.
The next day upon my arrival in Aberdeen,
after debarking from the train, I went inside
a coffee shop in the station. While waiting
in line to be served, another young man two
people in front of me began to shake and
to have a seizure. I managed to catch him
before his head hit the floor and held him
until it was over. Then two policemen showed up
and took over the situation.

Wed. Sept. 8   Largs, ~~the~~ Scotland
Returned to Largs yesterday late afternoon.
Went for a train ride up north to find Findhorn,
and Findhorn Park the intentional community there.
As the train was pulling out of one of the
stations after Largs, a newley boarded passenger,
a young man about twenty, while passing by
my seat stopped for a moment and began to
have a siezure. I imediately got up and as he
began to fall ~~~~ guided him gently to the
floor and held him. One of the passengers in
the forward part of the car (a nurse as it turned
out) came down the isle to assist me and
held his legs down, as he was flaying about
a bit. Then a doctor, who was in the next
forward car, showed up and soon the young
man was over the siezure and we helped
him up to a seat.
    The next day upon my arrival in Aberdeen
after debarking from the train I went inside
a coffee shop in the station and while waiting
in line to be served, another young man, two
people in front of me, began to shake and ~~~~
to have a siezure and I managed to catch him
before his head hit the floor and held him
untill it was over, and two policemen showed up
and took over the situation.

282

A week ago Monday, arrived at
Findhorn Park and signed up as a volunteer
there for a week and worked with a carpenter
by the name of Stephen Linturn, who was rebuilding
Eileen Caddy's original trailer (more like restoring
it). Cost me twenty-five pounds a day for the
privilege. It was truly a privilege to
have spent the time there, and with Stephen and
Eileen Caddy. Would have liked to have stayed
longer and perhaps will return one day to do
just that.
On Sunday past, Julie Salt, a Quaker I
met on my arrival in Forres last week,
came by and picked me up and gave me
a lift to a Quaker Meeting there which we
attended with seven others. After meeting
caught the train to Edinburgh, stayed the
night and the next day, back to Largs in the
evening.
Yesterday took the ferry to Cumbrae and
spent the day making Kandahar ready for the
winter. She sits high and dry next to a field
of cows on the edge of the Clyde, I'm saddened
at the thought of leaving her, so faithful she
has been to me, carrying me through

A week ago, ~~Tuesday~~ no Monday, arrived at Findhorn Park and signed up as a volunteer there for a week and worked with a carpenter by the name of Stephen Lintram who was rebuilding Eileen Caddy's original trailer (more like restoring it) cost me twenty five pounds a day for the privaledge and it was truley a privaledge to have spent the time there and with Stephen and Eileen Caddy. Would have liked to have stayed longer and prehaps will return one day to do just that.

On ~~saturday~~ ~~past~~, Julie Salt, a Quaker I met on my arrival in Forres last week, came by and picked me up and gave me a lift to a Quaker meeting there which we attended with ~~seven~~ others. After meeting caught the train to Edinburgh, stayed the night and the next day, back to Forres in the evening.

Yesterday took the ferry to Cumbrae and spent the day making Kandahar ready for the winter. She sits high and dry next to a field of cows on the edge of the Clyde, I'm saddned at the thought of leaving her, so faithfull she has been to me ~~carrying~~ carrying me through

284

thick and thin, overcoming my mistakes and
shortcomings. I sat in the cockpit one last
time before leaving, as the sun gave way to
a light sprinkle and thought about next summer
and returning, with Margi for a romantic adventure
here. I've been away for seventy-three days today.
Made arrangements with Jimmy's brother, Eric, for
a lift to Glasgow's airport tomorrow. He said
he would pick me up at eight in the morning and
I'm all packed and ready to go. Margi is going to
pick me up in Boston. Can't wait, can't wait,
can't wait, to see her!!!

Sept. 9, 1993 2:20 PM
Aboard Northwest Airlines high above the
North Atlantic more than halfway home now.
Hard to believe that what took me fifty-six days
to accomplish is only going to take five and
a half hours on this plane.
Didn't think I was going to get this far after
the ride to the airport this morning. Eric
picked me up ok, and with plenty of time, but
I am still feeling the effects of the ride in his
Ford Mustang, that he seems to drive with a

thick and thin, overcoming my mistakes and
shortcommings. I sat in the cockpit one last
time ~~before~~ leaving, as the sun gave way to
a light sprinkle and thought about next summer
and returning with Margi for a romatic adventure
here. I've been away for seventy three days today.
   Made arrangements with Jimmys brother Eric for
a lift to Glasgows airport tomorrow. ~~Eric~~ He said
he would pick me up at eight in the morning and
I'm all packed and ready to go. Margi is going to
pick me up in Boston. Can't wait, can't wait,
can't wait, to see her !!!.

_____

Sept. 9, 1993   2:20 PM
Aboard Northwest Airlines high above the
North Atlantic more than halfway home now.
Hard to believe that what took me fifty six days
to accomplish is only going to take five and
a half hours on this plane.
Didn't think I was going to get this far after
the ride to the airport this morning. Eric
picked me up ok and with plenty of time but
I am still feeling the effects of the ride in his
Ford Mustang, that he seems to drive with a

vengeance. I thought we would be killed at
any moment during the trip. I used to own one
of those Mustangs a '68 Fastback, with lots of horsepower
and drove it fast on occasion, but
not on the wrong side of the road!! Anyway,
I bet Eric got a kick out of scaring the hell
out of me and said have a nice trip with a big
smile on his face as he left me standing at the
curb in a cloud of rubber smoke.

9-10-93 3 PM
Bumble Bee Farm, Little Compton, RI.
We pass beneath the over hanging apple
bearing boughs. She drives, my heart is
heavy with the pain of leaving, although I
just arrived. My seventy-three day absence,
the longest period of separation for Margi and
I and yet I felt close to her the entire time.
For me my arrival back to the States was
a personal triumph. I was high on my
accomplishments, steady and focused.
Spending the night with her was awkward.
I felt a wall, a wall not there before.

287

vengence. I thought we would be killed at
any moment during the trip. I used to own one
of those Mustangs a "68" fastback with lots of horsepower ~~~~ and drove it fast on occasion, but
not on the wrong side of the road!! Anyway
I bet Eric got a kick out of scaring the ~~hell~~
out of me and said have a nice trip with a big
smile on his face ~~as he~~ left me standing at the
curb in a cloud of rubber smoke.

9-10-93   3:PM

Bumble "Bee" farm, Little Compton, R.I.
We pass beneath the over hanging apple
bearing boughs. She drives, my heart is
heavy with the pain of leaving, although I
just arrived. My seventy three day absents,
the longest period of seperation for Margi and
I and yet I felt close to her the entire time.
For me my arrival back to the states was
a personal triumph. I was high on my
accomplishments, steady and focused.
Spending the night with her was awkward,
I felt a wall, a wall not there before.

288

We bathed together and talked, I felt the wall,
We slept together and cuddled but there was
that wall. I stayed awake for hours, got up
for a while and read, returned to bed and laid
awake for more hours, up again, and I began
to let go of waiting for her to discuss the
wall. What ever it was between us was held
by her. I felt it but I had waited for months,
years even, to be able to be with her freely
and openly and close. Morning finally came
and she prepared some breakfast and brought
it into bed for me, kissed me and went down
the stairs to work the day at the farm.
It was early afternoon when she returned
home. I had managed to finally sleep some,
and woke to her voice. There was a lot of
energy around me from my trip home and
being with her in her bed after such a long
separation. She was quiet and a little tired
as she laid down be side me. I reached over
and felt her brow, welcomed her with a
kiss and noticed the moistness in her eyes,
she began to speak. Softly her words were
formed and spoken and softly my heart listened
as she revealed to me how difficult it was

We bathed together and talked, I felt the wall.
We slept together and cuddled but there was
that wall. I stayed awake for hours, got up
for awhile and read, returned to bed and lyed
awake for more hours, up again and I began
to let go of ~~the~~ waiting for her to discuss the
wall. What ever it was between us was held
by her. I felt it but I had waited for mouths,
years evan to be able to be with her freely
and openly and close. Morning, finally came
and she prepared some breakfast and brought
it into bed for me, kissed me and went down
the stairs to work the day at the farm.

   It was early afternoon when she returned
home. I had managed to finally sleep some,
and woke to her voice. There was a lot of
energy around me from my trip home and
being with her in her bed after such a long
seperation. She was quiet and a little tired
as she layed down beside me. I reached over
and felt her brow, welcomed her with a
kiss and noticed the moistness in her eyes,
she began to speak. Softly her words were
formed and spoken and softly my heart listened
as she revealed to me how diffacult it was

for her, the not knowing, the not knowing
if I was alive or would ever see and touch
me ever again.

How easy to get lost in fear,
When lost in someone we hold dear,
Loneliness holds life at bay,
Seems to stop the flow.
We struggle for escape,
And when we hear the serpents call,
How easily, our friend, we rape.

She tells me that she met a man,
The pain is swift and deep.
And of wanting to be held and felt.
And of her need to tell me now,
Not hold it in out of fear.
How hard this is for both of us,
A sickness creeps in as I hear her words.

Now maggots crawl,
where the sweet of love once filled my heart.

I don't know what to say. She drives.
I didn't know what to say, or do. I got sick
to my gut. All I could say was "Would you please
drive me to my sister's?" And I got up and got
dressed, and here we are driving.

for her, the not knowing, the not knowing
if I was alive or would ever see and touch
me ever again.

How easy to get lost in fear,
when lost in someone we hold dear.
Loneliness holds life at bay,
seems to stop the flow.
~~We~~ We struggle for escape,
And when we hear the Serpents call
How easily, ~~our~~ friend, We escape.

She tells me that she met a man.
(The pain is swift and deep.)
and of wanting to be held and felt.
and of ~~need~~ her need to tell me now
not hold it in out of fear.
How hard this is for both of us, a sickness
creeps in as I hear her words.

Now maggots crawl where the sweet of
love once filled my heart.
I don't know what to say. She drives.
I didn't know what to say, or do. I got sick to
my gut. All I could say was would you please
drive me to my sister's. And I got up and got
dressed and here we are driving.

292

My heartache is affecting my brain. It's
difficult to think. What's goin' on? Who am
I? Feeling disoriented, the scenery goes
by. The scenery I grew up with, the
scenery of my heart. The scenery is the
same but the scenery of my heart has changed,
the scenery of my heart feels blank, empty,
void. I can't speak. My throat feels tight.
I can't look at her. I'm frozen in fear. What's
wrong with me?

9-11-93 3 PM Brant Rock
The trip from Ltl. Compton* to Middleboro*
yesterday was in silence. We arrived about
four o'clock. A civil visit. Aileen, my
sister, two years younger than me, had
met Margi before. And after giving me
a huge hug and kiss on the cheek and
me hugging her the same, greeted Margie
in the same way. Ten or fifteen minutes
of small talk later, I suggested
to Margi that it was getting late
and she graciously made her departure.
I walked her to her car and said goodbye.
But I don't want to say goodbye to her!

* Ltl Compton, RI
* Middleboro, MA

My heart-ache is affecting my brain. It's difficult to think. What's going on. Who am I! Feeling disoriented, the scenary goes by. The scenary I grew up with, the scenary of my heart. The scenary is the same but the scenary of my heart has changed, the scenary of my heart feels blank, empty, void. I can't speak, my throat feels tight, I can't look at her, I'm frozen in fear, what's wrong with me?

9-11-93   3. PM Brant Rock

The trip from Ftl.Compton to Middlebough yesterday was in silence. We arrived about four oclock, a civil visit. Aileen, my sister, two years younger than me, had met Margi before, and after giving me a huge hug and kiss on the cheek and me hugging her the same, greeted Margi in the same way. Ten or fifteen minutes ~~the~~ of small talk later I suggested to Margi that it was getting late and she graciously made her departure. I walked her to her car and said goodbye. But I don't want to say goodbye to her!

Yet I have to stop thinking about her.
I have to stop seeing her. It hurts too bad.
There was such a security in her love and
now such a lonely abyss.
Brant Rock is a meditative place for me,
anyplace there's an ocean and a beach,
maybe it transforms me back to my youth
in Dennisport, on the Cape, where I had
the whole summer to pretty much do what
I please, fish, crab, swim. At ten or
eleven, I would collect sea-clam shells
on the beach, paint scenes of boats and
lighthouses and fish and crabs on the
shells, sell them for a nickel a-piece.
and reward myself with candy and gum
and ice creams and sodas. And my sister
Aileen at eight or nine, tagging along
and helping out. Some times are worth
remembering. I must concentrate on
good things. Good times, good memories,
I must think happy thoughts, but
difficult, I must not show the heartache
of nineteen months ago when
she found another man, or nine or ten
or who ever. I was over all that, over it

Yet I have to stop thinking about her.
I have to stop seeing her. It hurts to bad.
There was such a security in her love and
now such a lonely abyss.
Brant Rock is a medatative place for me,
anyplace there's an ocean and a beach,
maybe it transforms me back to my youth
in Dennis Port, on the Cape, where I had
the whole summer to pretty much do what
I please, fish, crab, swim. At ten or
eleven I would collect sea-clam shells
on the beach, paint scenes of boats and
light houses and fish and crabs on the
shells, sell them for a nickle a-piece
and reward myself with candy and gum
and ice cream and sodas. And my sister
Eileen at eight or nine, tagging along
and helping out. Sometimes are worth
remembering. I must concentrate on
good things. Good times, good memories,
I must think happy thoughts, but
dificult, I must not show the heart-
ake of nineteen months ago when
she found another man or nine or ten
or who ever. I was over all that, over it

296

when I left on the journey to Scotland.
I thought she had played out the field
and decided on being with me. I felt
so close to her and felt she so close
to me. I didn't want to leave then,
maybe I should have stayed. No, it
was too late then, I already had my
mind made up, my mind was set, I
had to go through with it. It was
only going to be a month and she was
going to fly over when I got there.
Something I had to prove to myself.
I wanted the adventure. I had to do it,
then especially, otherwise, yes, I could
have stayed and maybe settled down
with her and then later had regrets, she
might have had feelings later too
for talking me out of it. Who knows?
Who knows anything? I thought
I knew lots of things but turns
out I don't know a damn thing
about <u>anything</u>!!! Especially <u>anybody</u>!!!

> How many sounds of "fool"
> Must dance upon the brain?
> How many tears must flow,
> Before I call the game?

when I left on the journey to Scotland. I thought she had played out the field and decided on being with me. I felt so close to her and felt she so close to me. I didn't want to leave then, maybe I should have stayed. No it was to late then, I already had my mind made up, my mind was set, I had to go through with it. It was only going to be a month and she was going to fly over when I got there. Something I had to prove to myself, I wanted the adventure. I had to do it, then especially, otherwise yes, I could have stayed and maybe settled down with her and then later had regrets, she might have had feelings later too for talking me out of it, who knows, who knows anything, I thought I knew lots of things but turns out I don't know a damn thing about anything !!! Especially anybody !!!

How many sounds of "fool," must dance upon the brain, How many tears must flow, Before I call this game.

GLOSSARY

Amidships

In the center of the vessel; with reference to her length or breadth.

Beanbag chair

A large bean bag made of vinyl fabric and filled with foam pellets as of polystyrene, that shift about to fit one's body.

Beam

The beam of a ship or boat is its width at the widest point.

Beat-beating

Going toward the direction of the wind, by alternate tacks.

Cabin sole

The floor of the cockpit or cabin.

Cone or drogue

A device trailed behind a vessel on a long line in heavy weather, used to slow the vessel and keep the hull perpendicular to the waves.

Dodger

A frame supported canvas structure which covers part of the cockpit, providing partial protection from rain, spray, snow and wind.

Gale

Wind 39-54 mi. per hr.

Genoa jib

A large headsail which overlaps the mainsail. Used on sloops, ketches and yawls.

Hanking

Hanked on sails are sails that must be hauled down and up manually.

Hove-to

Fixing the helm and sail positions so that the boat does not actively have to be steered. Commonly used for a "break", such as lunch or to tend to other issues on the boat.

Hurricane

Wind above 72 mi. per hr.

Jib sheet

In sailing, a sheet is a line (rope, cable or chain) used to control the moveable corner(s) (clews) of a sail.

Knot (kt)

A knot is a unit of speed equal to one nautical mile per hour, approximately 1.151 mph.

Longliner

A commercial fishing boat that uses fishing gear typically composed of 100 fathom (600 foot/183 meter) leaded ground line that has an anchor and float line attached to each end. Baited hooks are attached at regular intervals along the ground line with short leaders or gangions.

Main; main sail

The principal sail of a vessel. A sail located behind the main mast of a sailing vessel.

One banger

A motor having one cylinder.

Port reach

In sailing, when the wind is coming over the port (left) side of the boats beam.

Red Nun

"Nun" buoys have a conical shape, are red in color and are even numbered. They define the starboard or right side of the channel.

Reef

In sailing, is a manoeuvre to reduce the area of a sail.

Rumb line

The path of a ship that maintains a fixed compass direction, shown on a map or chart as a line crossing all meridians at the same angle.

Rode

Another term for the anchor line.

Roller reefing

Roller reefing involves rolling or wrapping the sail around a wire, foil, or spar to reduce the sail exposure to the wind.

Running

Sailing on a direct downwind course.

Running rigging

The term for the rigging of a sailing vessel that is used for raising, lowering and controlling the sails - as opposed to the standing rigging, which supports the mast and other spars.

Seaway

A rough or heavy sea.

Starboard reach

In sailing, when the wind is coming over the starboard or right side of the boats beam.

Stiff breeze

A strong wind, 25-38 mi. per hr.

Trawler

Also called a dragger. A commercial fishing vessel designed to operate fishing trawls. Trawls are fishing nets that are pulled along the bottom of the sea or in midwater at a specified depth.

Up haul

A rope used for hauling up a boats sail.

Whole gale

Wind 55-72 mi. per hr.

Wing and wing

The situation of a fore-and aft vessel when she is going dead before the wind, with her foresail (jib) on one side and her mainsail on the other.

WHY I PUBLISHED

When I returned from Scotland in September 1993, I put this journal away out of sight, doing my best to move on with my life. Over the years, when I came across it now and then, it reminded me of feelings I would rather forget, and I'd tell myself that one day I could look forward to realizing a freedom over my past. Publishing this journal and sending it out freely to the Universe is, for me, that realization.

ABOUT THE AUTHOR

Bill Howland grew up in Hanson, a small agricultural town in southeastern Massachusetts.

Bill is mostly a contrarian, a nature believed to be inherited. Since this put him at odds with the notions of authority he left tenth grade and joined the Navy in 1962, to make a life of his own.

The Navy and the circumstance of his parents divorce while in boot camp reinforced his self-reliance, and the freedom and power of the sea reinforced his adventurous spirit.

Having fulfilled his obligation to his country he declined the offer to reenlist. Instead, he ventured to Brooklyn, New York, signed up for the Merchant Marine, joined the International Seafarers Union and shipped out of Port Elizabeth, New Jersey, on a container ship bound for Scotland and Germany.

Returning to the States, he was employed with a steel erection company in Massachusetts, met his future wife in New Hampshire, was married in 1969, and relocated to Fort Pierce, Florida, where his son, John Emerson, was born in 1970.

During the gas crisis of 1974 and the sharp decline in building, he moved his family to the west coast of Florida, near Clearwater, and found work as a cabinet maker. In 1975, they welcomed their daughter, Shelby Ann, into the world.

In 1980, his marriage dissolved. He returned to Massachusetts, settling in Sandwich, on Cape Cod in 1981, with his children and his new mate, Sally, and her six children.

Two years after this journal was written, he met Elayna. They reside together in Pembroke, Massachusetts, where he practices his trade as a carpenter-cabinet maker.

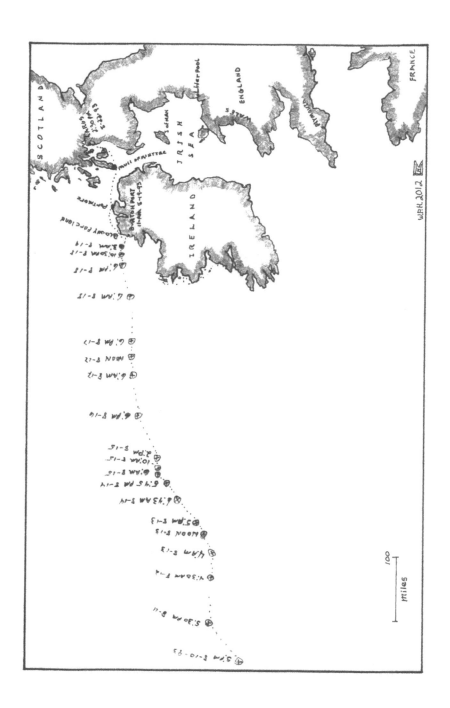